DAUGHTERS *of* FEMINISTS

DAUGHTERS *of* FEMINISTS

Rose L. Glickman

St. Martin's Press   New York

The names of all the daughters and some identifying details in this book have been changed for reasons of privacy.

The author gratefully acknowledges permission to reprint from the following previously copyrighted material:

Excerpt from "Words on Words" by Vaclav Havel from the *New York Review of Books,* copyright © 1990 by NYREV, Inc.

Excerpt from *On Lies, Secrets, and Silence* by Adrienne Rich. Copyright © 1979 by Adrienne Rich. Reprinted by permission of W. W. Norton & Company, Inc.

Library of Congress Cataloging-in-Publication Data

Glickman, Rose L.
    Daughters of feminists: young women with feminist mothers talk about their lives/Rose Glickman.
        p.   cm.
    ISBN 0-312-09778-6
    1. Feminists—United States—Family relationships. 2. Daughters—United States—Attitudes. 3. Mothers and daughters—United States.
    I. Title.
HQ1421.G55   1993
306.874'3—dc20   93-24286
                                                  CIP

Design by Judith A. Stagnitto

First Edition: October 1993

10 9 8 7 6 5 4 3 2 1

To my mother, Clara Burd, in memory,
and to my daughter Eve.

CONTENTS

· · · · · · · ·

ACKNOWLEDGMENTS

. . . .

We cannot tell the precise moment when friendship is formed. As in filling a vessel drop by drop, there is at last a drop which makes it run over; so in a series of kindnesses there is at last one which makes the heart run over.

—JAMES BOSWELL,
BOSWELL'S LIFE OF JOHNSON, 1777

Although collegiality and friendship have many characteristics in common, often what we demand in one, we are prepared to relinquish in the other. I feel particularly blessed that my colleagues and friends are one and the same. I have benefited from the best of each relationship.

Acknowledging my sole responsibility for this book, I am grateful that my colleague-friends unswervingly cheered me on even as they boldly snorted at this or that formulation, rolled their eyes in disbelief that I could make this or that statement, patiently and repeatedly applied the red pencil to mishmash, simplemindedness, or pomposity.

To Zelda Bronstein, Gabrielle Burton, and Maxine

Lange, profound gratitude for all of the above, for a lot of laughs, and much, much more.

To Lucy Kaplan, Kenneth Kann, Joan Levinson, Isabel Marcus, Molly Rosenhan, David Rosenhan, and John Spier, for readings, ideas, conversations, advice about this book, and other fine things over the years.

To Deborah Ott and the other women and men, too numerous to name, for generous help in finding daughters from all over the maps of geography, race, ethnic and class origin.

To Maureen Baron and Anne Savarese, my editors, and Charlotte Sheedy, my agent, for bestowing on me their skills and their kindness.

To the feminist mothers for agreeing to let me interview their daughters, and for throwing in their hurrahs for the project as well.

To the daughters for their time, their enthusiasm, their honesty. Each interview was pleasure and enlightenment.

To my own flesh-and-blood daughter, Eve Glickman. She knows why.

ROSE L. GLICKMAN

BERKELEY, CALIFORNIA

A few years ago my friend Isabel and I, driving home at night in a howling Buffalo storm, diverted ourselves with some talk about our daughters. The interior of an automobile is not what I normally think of as a place for a great conversation. But somehow the subject of our daughters was like a buffer between us and the sleet pounding on the window, the ice beneath the wheels, the lurching traffic. Our daughters, both twenty-five at the time, had grown up on the same block in Berkeley, California, had gone to the same schools, and had many friends in common. Isabel and I exchanged anecdotes about our daughters' childhoods, gossiped about their friends, reported on what our girls were doing now, bragged a bit about their virtues, and then, in the odd intimacy of the beleaguered car, admitted to some despair and much astonishment. Had we really expected them to grow up feminists just like us?

The answer, of course, was yes. Timidly we asked each other—have they? Ruefully we concluded, well, no—but not exactly no. They surpass us, as we had hoped they would, in strength and confidence as women. We allowed that they have indeed absorbed much of our perspective on what it is to be a woman in this society and what it should be. But some issues that seem to us absolutely central to feminism are at best uninteresting, at worst irrelevant to them. I still grind my teeth when I recall my daughter's adolescent dismissal of my hortatory lectures: "Lighten up, Mama, lighten up." What a peculiar mishmash—our daughters. Someone should explore this, I thought, when we parted. We should know what has happened to the daughters of feminists.

I come to this project from observing my own daughter, her friends, my students; from comparing daughters with feminist friends in conversations simultaneously proud, admiring, disappointed, wondering, amazed, perplexed. I come to this project out of irritation with the media image that reduces today's young adult women to a collective Big Chill of feminism. Like most media generalizations, it represents something, but not everything. It reveals a truth for some and a simplistic and banal distortion for many others. It purports to reveal as much by omission as by inclusion; by whom it chooses or neglects to interview, quote, portray; by, as Adrienne Rich puts it, "willful ignorance, reductiveness, caricature, distortion, trivialization." It obscures a rich and intricate medley of daughters' responses to their mothers' feminism.

It would be folly to assume some determining mechanistic parental influence on the daughters of feminists. God knows—conservative parents produce radical children, radical parents turn out conservative children, hippie parents spawn suburban paragons, and traditional women rear feminist daughters. Otherwise nothing would ever change and the women's movement would not have been reborn in the late 1960s.

The testimony to that movement includes women who enroll in the Women's Studies programs at American universities, who work in the law offices, the primary and secondary schools, the universities, the women's health collectives and shelters, public and private institutions of every description, and in places where women were not to be found before. It includes a new sensitivity, however besieged, to women's issues in the courts, among legislators, in literature. In all the crevices of society one finds many women who, despite the transformation the movement has undergone (and they with it), acknowledge the influence of feminism and continue its battles in their private and public lives. Even the backlash among women, men, and institutions is a testimony to the significant changes wrought by a movement now much altered, surely endangered, but not extinct.

One cannot always easily distinguish by external behavior and attitudes the women whose mothers were feminists from those whose mothers were not. In a profound sense all women roughly between the ages of eighteen and thirty-five, whether they embrace or reject feminism, are the daughters of feminism, heir to its struggles, failures, and successes; inheritors, willy-nilly, of the heroic phase of the modern women's movement.

But this book is about the journey of those women whose mothers called themselves feminists. It is about women influenced not by what was in the wind, but by the immediate and intimate example and teachings of mothers pioneering new ways to be a woman in the world. Like all journeys it is a dynamic process, always in flux, shaping and responding at the same time. I know what it was like to be a feminist mother. I would like to know what was it was like to be the child of a mother actively engaged in redrawing the human map, simultaneously catapulted forward by a new consciousness and restrained by the ponderous weight of traditions no longer satisfactory but secure.

How did (and do) the daughters experience the mothers' struggle, and what elements of it have they absorbed as they draw their own cognitive map? We will pause at important signposts in the life of the mothers' generation, examining how the daughters regard sexuality and femininity, work, family, and friendship. We will unravel public and private image and reality, the interaction of race, ethnicity, and gender, exploring the decisions the daughters make about their lives and how they explain them.

The daughters who accept their mothers' dreams, expectations, and formulations have not done so wholesale. They take a nip here, a tuck there, rearrange and reformulate the legacy into a pattern of their own. Even those daughters who question their mothers' feminist perspective and struggle, who espouse more traditional attitudes, who are sometimes angry with and critical of their mothers—even they do not speak, dream, anticipate as I did at their age in the 1950s. The interesting questions are what the daughters reject, what they accept, how they juggle the elements. Each version has something in common with the mother's version, with the version of other daughters, and each version has something of its own. It is precisely the versions, what they have in common with each other and with their mothers', how they are idiosyncratic, that this book addresses.

Daughters of Feminists is the result of interviews with fifty women whose mothers called themselves feminists from the daughters' early childhood. The interviews took place mainly in four geographical areas: the San Francisco Bay Area, Chicago, western New York State, and New York City. The daughters did not necessarily grow up where they live now, a happenstance for which I am grateful. Feminism provided women with a community of common perspectives and goals, but the particular social climate of each geographical community influenced the experience of feminism for both mothers and daughters.

When it was possible, I spoke briefly to the mother to verify that she considered herself a feminist and to make sure she had no objections to having her daughter (or daughters) interviewed. I did not inquire into the particular brand of feminism that the mothers espoused. The debates within the women's movement are not the issue, and whether the mother was a socialist feminist, a radical feminist, a cultural feminist, or whatever, is irrelevant to my inquiry. Nor, as I went about talking to daughters, did I ask whether the mother had been actively involved in feminist causes. But as it turned out, every mother without exception "walked her talk," as one daughter expressed it. The mothers were and are practicing feminists, experimenting, groping, striving to realize their convictions and dreams in their private and public lives. Many are well known in their geographical, professional, or cultural communities, but I avoided the daughters of women famous, or notorious, on a national level. Fame, or notoriety, are exceptional experiences; I was looking for the common experience.

I also ruled out daughters whose mothers' lives can surely be described as feminist, but who reject the label. Once, in my search for Latina daughters, I spoke with the head of a Latina women's health collective. She said she couldn't help me because "although we have the consciousness, in our culture we don't use that word." The consciousness without the word is not what I'm looking for.

Often I came away from an interview simultaneously depressed and exhilarated—and for the same reason. The daughters take as their birthright things that I have struggled for all my life—and I'm *still* not there and probably never will be. I exult for the daughters and feel a bit sad for myself. I think the daughters enjoyed and learned from the interviews as well. Many thanked me for bringing up issues that they had never consciously explored or for provoking them to think more deeply about issues they had long taken for granted.

I regard this book as a form of oral history. I believe that a qualitative narrative is the best way to explore the transmission of a world view from mother to daughter. My goal is to ferret out and understand the varieties of the daughters' reinterpretations of feminism, to explore the nuances, not to reduce the contemporary "postfeminist" to a compact collection of categories and to assign percentages to them. That is why, as you read, you will encounter adjectives like *many, some,* and *few,* instead of percentages. The kinds of questions I ask cannot be answered with a simple yes or no.

I have tried to be intellectually rigorous in the design of my search, the questions I ask, and to have avoided as much as possible guiding and prejudicing the responses of my informants.

CHAPTER ONE

The Word

The point I am trying to make is that words are a mysterious, ambiguous, ambivalent, and perfidious phenomenon. They are capable of being rays of light in a realm of darkness. . . . They are equally capable of being lethal arrows. Worst of all, at times they can be the one and the other. And even both at once.

—VACLAV HAVEL, "WORDS ON WORDS," 1990

In my sixteenth year, 1949, I underwent a profound crisis. You wouldn't have known it to look at me. My school performance was outstanding, my social skills honed to virtuosity. Life was a cornucopia of telephone calls, dates, overflowing dance cards. Because the boys liked me, my status among my girlfriends was secure. I worked relentlessly at being popular.

The nature of the crisis was that I discovered something for which I had no name. I—the budding wordsmith, the mistress of the wisecrack, the glib author of the school newspaper's gossip column (identity revealed only at graduation), the voracious reader and denizen of

1

the public library—was struck dumb. The world had turned inside out, but I had no vocabulary to explain it either to myself or to others. In retrospect it is difficult to sort out what tormented me more—the discovery itself or the betrayal by that language which had been a taproot of discovery, pleasure, and success.

To this day the event that triggered a year of wordless depression saddens me. Sheila Crane was a semester behind me. Sheila was popular, too. I scarcely knew her and didn't want to know her, for her popularity unfolded in mocking rhymes devoted to her charms, snide whispers behind hands in locker rooms, salacious rumors that followed her in the school's corridors. Sheila had a "reputation." Everyone knew she was always ready to service the boys, not with sexual intercourse—that would have been bad enough—but with an act so mysterious, so aberrant, so vile, that my girlfriends and I had no word for it. (Remember, this was 1949.)

One day the boys in our crowd, bursting with adolescent triumph, let it be known that they had assembled in a room with Sheila and persuaded her to perform this act on each boy serially. My own boyfriend had been present. I reeled from the shock of betrayal and confusion. How was I to hold on to this boyfriend? Our own gentle, tentative sexual explorations in the name of young love, or what I thought was love, couldn't compete with the Sheilas of this world. Nor did I want to. Look at the price Sheila paid for her popularity. I hope that in her adult life she transcended the hunger and self-abasement of her high school days. I even felt compassion for her at the time, but yet again words—and courage—eluded me.

The gloom of my boyfriend's disclosure and my inability to articulate it seeped into all the crevices of my life. Everything around me seemed tainted by humiliation for women. I went to a musical review in which Eartha Kitt startled and delighted the audience by exposing a perfect breast at the high point of her performance. My heart like a stone in my chest, I laughed and crowed with the audience. Eartha Kitt was popular. In the apartments and on the streets of my working-class neighborhood, I saw the women through a new lens: they were careworn, depressed, shabby in spirit as well as appearance. I conjured up their lives, not in words but in images—pictures of incessant washing, cleaning, feeding, nurturing, self-denial, unrewarded by male admiration. They were not popular. The better coiffed, better dressed and shod women that occasionally crossed my line of vision in the flesh or on magazine pages seemed no better off.

I made a powerful decision in the course of that dismal year: I would not be like the other women, neither the Sheilas and the Earthas (who in my adolescent angst I indiscriminately lumped together) nor the servile, unrewarded mothers, aunts, neighbors. It was not a sisterly decision. But my depression abated and I learned to control the anxiety that lurked on the periphery of consciousness. I did not so easily relinquish the desire to be popular—with the boys and later the men—but now it would be on my own terms. I would have a life that transcended it all—domesticity, dependence, sexual pandering, and humiliation. I was a nascent queen bee. It was a lonely business.

When I was thirty-two, the single parent of a two-year-old daughter, I found a name for that agonizing discovery: sexism. Other words tumbled forth in exhilarating, joyful abundance. The rebirth of the women's movement supplied the words, the names, the syntax to help me comprehend and articulate the unvoiced perceptions that had haunted me for sixteen years. I was no longer mute and isolated. I had words and I had company. There was even a proud word to describe what I was—a feminist.

Every feminist of my generation has a version of that story, give or take a few years, substitute one detail for another, another genesis, another timetable. While there were many roads to feminism, they converged with the discovery of a vocabulary and a community that inspired or validated the quest to replace humiliation with dignity, self-sacrifice with self-realization, dependence with autonomy. Feminism called for a reevaluation of women's traditional reality, images, and roles.

The passage by Vaclav Havel that begins this chapter could have been designed to describe the feminist sensitivity to the interplay between words and the social construction of gender, to the importance of naming, to the word not only as reflection of reality but as a way to transform reality as well. The women's movement has explored the significance of language, taking it far beyond the level of academic literary exercise into the whole social and cultural fabric. Feminists have redefined old words and invented new ones, often irritating to the linguistically fastidious but appropriate to altered perceptions and to challenges of what one of the daughters I interviewed calls "the old country."

Our daughters have a whole arsenal of words that we lacked in our formative years and sometimes well into adulthood. If we credit the power of the word, it is fitting to begin a book on daughters of feminists by examining how they regard the word *feminist*. As with every element of the mothers' legacy, the daughters' interpretations reveal a multilayered, complex, untidy reality.

Well into every interview I ask, "Would you call your-self a feminist?" I am prepared for any response except the one some give: "I really don't know what it means." The question, after all, follows a long discussion of the mothers' feminism, what it was like to grow up in a feminist household, and a host of issues directly and tangentially related to feminism. Daughters who answer this way are well aware of the issues and they speak with pride and admiration of their mothers. Indeed, at other points in the interviews, they come up with definitions of feminism that would make their mothers proud.

It soon becomes clear that this puzzling answer always comes from daughters who are especially tentative about their lives in general. Their plans for tomorrow are as vague as their aspirations for ten years hence. One plan, one fantasy after another, tumbles forth without shape or chronology. They are trying on hats in the narratives they devise for me as well as in their daily lives. They are groping for identity, for concrete goals. To be a feminist is one among many options for them, because they do not recognize it as a process, as a perspective that informs other choices. They interpret the word as an end in itself. And when they say they don't know what "feminist" means, they are saying they don't know what it means for them: "I'm not saying I don't want to be a feminist, and maybe at some point in my life I'll say *yes,* I know I am. But I guess I have no reason to say that I'm a feminist yet."

The phrase "I'm not a feminist, but . . ." has become a clichéd description of how women in general think about women's issues. The daughters of feminists, rarely prepared to disavow the label of feminist, have their own guarded way of describing themselves. The daughters say "I *am* a feminist, but . . .". Certain consistent themes emerge from their responses, as well as certain consistent strategies. The most common strategy, which is what I am calling the way many daughters choose to couch their responses, is to tell me how *other* people perceive the word. I never ask about other people's opinions of the word, but it precedes or follows the answer so often that I begin to wonder whether the daughters have colluded in writing a script.

Other people, they tell me uneasily, associate feminists with lesbians. It is an obstinate underlying hum, a dissonance that augurs cacophony. And often the feminist/lesbianism connection and attribution to the outside world go hand in hand. "What they express to me," Jenna says, "is that the feminist is a dyke. Not a lesbian, but a dyke, a mean woman, a harsh woman, an ugly woman." Jenna, twenty-one, talks to me in the book-strewn living room of the brown-shingle house in which she and her older sister grew up. It is the Christmas break at the northern California university where she studies biology. "These days in the Women's Studies program, unless you're a lesbian you're not considered a feminist. You've got to be a lesbian," she says. Jenna has many lesbian friends and she reminisces about her lesbian nanny with enormous affection. "I think it's fine. That's the way it is for some people, the way it *should* be for some people." But while she affirms her own feminism without hesitation, she squirms in the public eye: "I'm against the image that they're portraying. I don't want them to look at me and see me that way."

Colette, a twenty-two-year-old African American daughter, is in medical school. She calls herself a feminist, which she defines as "someone who's proud to be a woman, who recognizes her own and other women's capabilities. To me, it's completely positive. But people think that feminists are trying to run everything, to cut males out of society. Or that they're lesbians. There are people who think that if you love women, you must hate men." That's why before Colette publicly identifies herself as a feminist, "I have to find out what it means to the person who's asking."

Renata, however, is indifferent to the reciprocal connection that "others" make between the feminist and the lesbian. "If someone thinks I'm a lesbian because I call myself a feminist, I just laugh. Unless that person is prepared to hear me, I don't even bother to explain. I think, 'You just don't get it.' I just shrug it off."

Renata is exceptional. Most of the heterosexual daughters are not prepared to embrace the battle cry that Del Martin and Phyllis Lyon report in their book *Lesbian/Woman*:

> As one (heterosexual) NOW member put it to us, "I believe deeply that female sexuality is a key issue in the women's movement. Until every woman is able to say, 'Okay, so you think I'm a Lesbian. Fuck you—I will neither affirm nor deny it,' the women's movement will go nowhere.

The word *feminist* is no less charged for the lesbian daughters. Hilary, twenty-eight, lives with her partner and their fourteen-month-old son. She came out when she was sixteen. Hilary calls herself a feminist, but not easily: "When I was growing up, *feminist* was almost a bad word. To say the word was to instigate an argument." I ask her why it is easier to reveal her homosexuality, which, I assume, also provokes some negative responses. "If you're a lesbian, you're a lesbian." She shrugs. "It's not a code of belief." The problem for Hilary is that "*feminist* is always a word that someone else has defined. If I tell someone I'm a feminist, that person has a little code word in mind. To people who've worked very hard on feminist issues, I haven't done enough to justify calling myself a feminist, and to conservative people—well, they say, 'Oh, she's just a feminist,' and they dismiss me."

No matter how many ways I introduce the issue of homosexuality to the heterosexual daughters, it does not elicit moral judgment, personal revulsion, condescension, or disapproval of any sort. Homosexuality has been demystified for these women, mainly through exposure. Some have lesbian mothers or sisters, all have gay and lesbian friends and acquaintances. They regard homosexuality as part of the natural order. Why, when they identify themselves as feminists, are they so concerned that others associate it with lesbianism?

The truth is that the word *lesbian* is rarely used in heterosexual society solely as a definition of sexual preference. It is a metaphor—for "man-hating" and "male-bashing," for fanaticism, for separatism. It is from these connotations that the daughters wish to dissociate themselves.

Some daughters speak directly to the nuances. Amelia is twenty-six. Her mother is a feminist therapist and an activist in women's issues. Some years ago Amelia's older sister publicly announced her homosexuality. Amelia regards her sister's coming out as a wonderful, affirmative act because the sister was transformed from a miserable, depressed adolescent into a strong and happy adult. Amelia considers her sister her best friend. "I've never said, 'Pleased to meet you, I'm a feminist,' " she says, laughing. "But I am, I am. How could I be otherwise, growing up in my family? But that word has frightening connotations for a lot of men—and for women, too. It sort of means that you're righteous, that you're independent, that you can take on the world, that you're powerful, that you're as much a person as any male."

"Are these desirable qualities?" I ask.

"Definitely good qualities. But righteousness isn't a good thing when you're a female."

"Why is that?"

"Because if you're righteous, if you're a feminist, people see you not as a person with an opinion, but as a bitch. You're a bitch because you stick up for yourself. And nobody wants to be a bitch."

Does the strategy of attributing opinions to the world at large mask attitudes that the daughters themselves hold, but feel embarrassed about expressing? I think not. For these daughters the problem is how to call themselves feminists in a world that selectively and disapprovingly defines the word to exclude everything but the most dramatic and extreme elements. They tenaciously refuse to distance themselves from the label, but it causes them enormous discomfort. Nobody wants to be a bitch. Listen to how Mia wrestles with her internal and external demons.

Mia Atkins, age nineteen, is the fourth of five daughters in a family known for its feminism in a very conservative community. She and her sisters were relentlessly singled out in school, teased by classmates, and harassed by teachers. "In high school teachers would say something sexist and then turn to me—'Well, Mia, aren't you going to say something?' It was really unfair of them. But it happened all through high school."

"How did you feel about it?" I ask.

"I felt bad about it. I wished that I didn't have that reputation."

Mia's was relieved to shed the "baggage of all those sisters and that reputation" when she left home for college. During the first year, "when someone would ask me if I'm a feminist, my immediate reaction was to run away and say no, no, no. It was so hard to take pride in it." To the extent that she revealed herself, it was as "the most wishy-washy, watered-down sort of feminist. I just expressed normal beliefs against racism, poverty, sexism. I just said that everyone should have basic rights." She describes how, reluctant and uncertain, she eventually was flushed out and pegged as a radical advocate of "the women's thing."

I'd written a paper in which I alternated he and she as the neutral pronoun. Everyone in the class argued against me, saying that it was ridiculous, confusing, stupid. Then later in the year, a guy in the dormitory asked me to read his paper. In it he kept using the word *man*. I said, "Man? What do you mean— man? You mean humankind." And he said, "Oh, that's a nonissue, just a stupid thing that women think up to make trouble."

Other students, in fact the entire floor, drifted into the room and soon they were engaged in a boisterous debate—without Mia. "I just removed myself from the discussion because I was so annoyed." She reaped a modest reward: A week later the fellow student apologized to her and thanked her for enlightening him. Still, her first year at college was a slow, painful gathering of strength.

I didn't want to say anything at first. I didn't want to be conspicuous or offensive—offensive, quote-unquote. To be a feminist was like a scarlet *W*. I didn't want to be singled out. It was a burden. But this year I'm beginning to think, hey, feminist issues are totally important to me, and I'm on the right side. I don't have to be defensive anymore. So now I take more risks. Now when people ask me that question I turn it on them—I say, "Of course, aren't you?"

For a few daughters the problem is simpler. They come close to accepting the world's verdict that to be a feminist means to hate men, to be fanatical and strident. Nor do they regard these characteristics as the private property of feminists. These characteristics smack of an agenda that rejects established values in general (rarely defined), that is radical or liberal (often used interchangeably). Yes, they would call themselves feminists as long as it is clear that they are not *that* kind of feminist.

When I call to ask Jane's mother, a feminist theologian, whether I may interview her daughter, she warns me that I might find something unexpected. Jane, twenty-eight, is a full-time mother. Her young son is at school, her infant daughter is asleep in the next room. The room we sit in is littered with toys, unfolded laundry, stacks of unopened mail, cups half-filled with cold tea. Jane says she cannot control the chaos by herself, and her husband is not very "helpful." Both of them are ideologically opposed to paid household help. She explains that she would call herself something between a traditionalist and a raging feminist, which to her is "someone who hates men so much that they don't even spell the word *woman* with man at the end, somebody who really hates men and wants to be separate."

Separatism means something quite literal for Jane. It is unacceptable to her because she does not "hate men" and is therefore not prepared to relegate them to the periphery of women's lives. For others, separatism is more nuanced. Nina, twenty-five, worries that feminism introduces a divisive note into other important goals. Nina works as an environmentalist. Her mother is a lesbian and Nina wonders about the possibility of sexual and love relationships with women for herself, although until now she has had only heterosexual relationships.

"Would you call yourself a feminist?"

"Oh yes," she replies without hesitation. Then she pauses. "Well, actually, I have a problem with the way feminism is manifested in our world. I've done a lot of antinuclear work with the Livermore Action Group . . . Diablo Canyon, Vanderbrook Air Force Base, and I also lived at the Puget Sound Women's Peace Camp. I think that feminism is really valuable for women to empower themselves through other women, but I draw the line at separatism. I feel very, very strongly about that, especially when you're talking about world peace. I guess I want it to be clear that I'm a feminist, but not a separatist."

Does this amount to a verification of Carolyn Heilbrun's lament that "even today, after two decades of feminism, young women shy away from an emphatic statement of anger at the patriarchy"? There is clearly a great deal to Heilbrun's observation. As we shall see when we explore the daughters' life experiences, anger is alive and well. But nobody wants to be a bitch—or a man-hater, a fanatic, a separatist. These words, like the word *feminist,* alienate men. In the daughters' ruminations about their place in the feminist spectrum, anxiety at the prospect of alienating men crops up repeatedly.

Why should we use a word that makes men uncomfortable, that does not welcome them? Why do we need a word that belongs to a bygone era? Adrienne succinctly sums it up. She is thirty-three, married, and the mother of a two-year-old girl. Even with a husband who shares some of the household work, she is frustrated by the conflict between parenting and her career, the constraints on involvement in work she loves and consequently on her professional achievement. She believes that "we were sold a bill of goods when we were told we could have families and full-time careers and be happy." But Adrienne still believes there is something better down the line—if we are careful not to alienate men. "Sometimes I feel that women look hysterical when they bring their demands to a larger, more political arena. That's counterproductive. There has to be a way to get around it. There *are* ways to make women's demands felt without alienating men. I think the most effective are a little bit manipulative. You know, infiltration. Within your own little family or the company you work for."

Some daughters, definitely in the minority, declare themselves feminists with no reservations. The word is theirs. Fully aware of the world's definition and disapproval, they simply don't give a damn. Antonia, the third of the five Atkins daughters, says, "That's who I am, a feminist. I get so angry at my women friends who have a problem with it. They say, 'Well, it has such a bad connotation,' and I say, 'Who cares? *You* don't have to accept the bad connotations.' "

Ellie is a graduate student in photography. When I interview her she is wearing baggy pants, boots, and a dazzling oversized shirt. Her thick black hair is cut in a short, spiky crown above her delicate features. Although her fellow students often assume she is a lesbian because of her unisex style of dressing and because she excels at the technical aspects of photography, she is untroubled: "I have enough to worry about in school without caring whether people think I'm gay." Vexed by the simplistic and distorted reduction of the feminist to some mythical "bra-burning lesbian militant of the sixties," Ellie accepts lesbianism and militancy as valuable and legitimate aspects of the women's movement. But what, she wonders, has happened to all the rest of it?

Ellie describes a talk show she watched on television that purported to represent the current state of feminism. "The women on it were all saying we have to listen to men, we don't want to intimidate men, we don't want to alienate men. And all I could think was—*too bad!* I don't care if we alienate them or not. It was really horrifying to see these women, my age or maybe a little older, who are really talking themselves out of all their rights, trying to rationalize settling for less." Ellie is not unique, but she is among the exceptions—the daughters whose struggle is not with "other people's" definitions, but with how to live their lives as feminists.

Most touching, and perhaps most affirming in a peculiar sort of way, are the daughters who embrace the word, but who feel they don't live up to it. For them it is not a designation they can claim simply because they inherited a feminist perspective from their mothers or even because they think or feel as feminists. They feel they have to earn the label.

By current standards, Amy is enormously successful. A highly skilled systems analyst, she recently left a firm when the sexist bias of her male boss obstructed a promotion she deserved. She willingly accepted a job with a lower salary in a firm that promises to reward her for her abilities and not punish her for her gender. At age thirty she is still earning so much that she is embarrassed to reveal her salary. Any feminist mother would celebrate a daughter like Amy, not only because she calls herself a feminist, not only for her skills and achievements, but also for her thoughtfulness, her sensitivity, her concern with human liberation, her sense of social responsibility in general.

For Amy, however, thinking the right thoughts is not enough. She talks about the periods in her life when she translated good thoughts into action, about her volunteer work for NARAL, her letter-writing campaigns, her donations of money to abortion rights advocates—how despite everything she feels guilty about not volunteering to be an escort at the abortion clinics on Saturday mornings. When she affirms her feminism she qualifies it with a sense of inadequacy. At work she does not know how to cope with the men who use sexist language or make jokes about women. Should she make a public statement or talk to them privately after the event? Does she avoid confrontation because she fears it will tarnish her image as a professional?

"I feel like I don't stand up enough for it. I don't know how to fight these battles in productive ways." Now, absorbed in work and a relationship with a man she will probably marry, she honors her commitment only by giving money to feminist causes. Her successes, her good life, she says ruefully, have tempered her zeal to honor the word and the cause in deeds. It feels to her like a betrayal. She and others like her question whether they are earning the privilege of calling themselves feminists.

"Feminist" is surely among those words that Havel says are equally capable of being "rays of light in a realm of darkness" or "lethal arrows" or both at once. So it was from the beginning. The women's movement kindled a backlash at the very moment of its rebirth in the late 1960s. Hostility, ridicule, trivialization were its ubiquitous fellow travelers. The movement also was immediately embroiled in internal polemics, in conflicts over definition, over sexuality, race and class, over strategy and tactics. Neither attack from without nor controversy within are new in the daughters' generation.

Yet the mothers of all persuasions and at every level, grass roots to top echelon, called themselves feminists. The word was not in dispute. If this were a random survey of the daughters' generation, it would not be surprising to find a bit of this and a bit of that in responses to the word. But the women I interviewed were deliberately chosen for their direct and intimate exposure to everything the word signified. Why are their responses to it so complicated?

More than two decades after the rebirth of feminism, the substance of the attacks and controversies has abated over some issues, intensified over others, and in some cases assumed new dimensions. Shaped in part by the very word we are examining, the economic, political, and cultural climate significantly altered as the daughters were growing up, and continues to do so as they move through the present and aspire to the future. It is time to remove the word from under the microscope. The daughters of feminists understand very well that the word was and is enmeshed in a social context. Indeed, they insistently remind me of this as they struggle to reconcile their mothers' legacy with their own experiences in their world. We may well mourn the transformation of a robust, exultant shout into a tentative whisper. The word is in trouble. But revealing as the nuances of acceptance, ambivalence, or rejection of a crucial word are, that is not the whole story.

The rest of the story unfolds as we explore the process of transmission from mother to daughter by example and by teaching; how daughters of feminists interpret the substance of the word *feminist* and the achievements it inspires in their daily lives; how their mothers' feminist perspective shapes their expectations and aspirations.

. . . .

CHAPTER TWO

The Legacy: Growing Up Feminist

I could have written much better if I had been interrupted much less, and should have proved altogether a more effective person had I not been obliged—and not only in my youth—to spend time and energy learning to believe in myself and my purposes despite the enervating influence of an Edwardian childhood. That you, who have been spared that particular battle, will live to see women ascend to heights of achievement hitherto undreamed of and make your own contribution to this future stage of a great revolution, is the constant and hopeful joy of

Your Mother
—VERA BRITTAIN TO HER DAUGHTER,
***LADY INTO WOMAN*, 1953**

"It's interesting to me that you're doing a book on daughters of feminists rather than daughters of just strong women. Why is that? I have

strong women friends whose mothers have done incredible things by themselves, but wouldn't call themselves
feminists," a daughter challenges me. Am I, she wonders,
undervaluing strong mothers who did not call themselves
feminists and their daughters as well?

There are and always have been women who have done
incredible things by themselves. Once we knew them by
name. Now it is a job and a half to keep track of their
names. We celebrate them. And we celebrate those, past
and present, whose names we do not and cannot know,
for whom survival was itself as great a feat as public
achievement. In both cases *by themselves* is the operative
phrase. I draw a circle, as it were, around the daughters
of women who call themselves feminists because they had
a different experience from isolated strong women and
their daughters. The mothers know it and the daughters
know it.

What was it like to grow up the daughter of a feminist?
To understand how and whether the mothers' feminist
perspective—imagined and lived—influences the daughters, and what it is that the daughters are reinterpreting,
we must get to know the daughters in their formative
years. If the days were long enough I might have interviewed the mothers as well. They would surely give the
story a different slant. For example, when I ask Holly
who did the shopping and cooking in her family, she says
that "once" her father cooked a meal because her mother
and grandmother were ill: "The meal made me sick."
She laughs. "My mom said this never really happened,
but that's my memory of it." Perhaps the incident did
not happen exactly as Holly now recalls it. Her memory
is not a perfect photograph but a pastiche of recollections
that add up to her statement, later in the interview, that

"my mother definitely took care of the domestic things."
As the daughters sift through their memories, we will get
to know the mothers as well.

The daughters' lens also illuminates fathers, when they
were present in the daughters' lives; extended kin, which
often include the mothers' feminist community; and the
immediate geographical community of the daughters'
childhood and adolescence. As for anyone, the material
and psychological events of daily life, the relationships
that shape a life, are tangled in national and global events.

When my own daughter was four years old, she delighted in skipping down the driveway early each morn-
ing to fetch the newspaper. She had just learned to read.
One day, holding up her pajama bottoms with one small
hand and clutching the newspaper in the other, she
breathlessly piped up that Martin Luther King had been
assassinated. Later that year her baby-sitter took her to
hear Robert Kennedy speak on our southern California
campus. In a few days he too was assassinated. Exactly
who these people were was probably not clear to her
then. But the assassination of people whose names pep-
pered adult conversations became a part of her world.
The Vietnam War and the menace of nuclear horror were
for her and her peers a subtext to daily life.

The mother, the family, and the community cannot be
isolated from national and global influences, especially in
the case of feminist families; it is in the very nature of
feminism to recognize that there is no "outside." That is
what it means to make the personal political. And regardless of the mothers' specific political persuasions, more
often than not the political was profoundly personal.
Feminism, after all, was brewed in the crucible of the civil
rights and antiwar movements. Let us then attempt to

unravel the intricate tapestry of mother, family, community, and national atmosphere of the daughters' feminist childhoods.

All of the mothers worked outside the home or, to be more precise, had careers. We find them in traditional women's fields, like nursing, elementary school teaching, social work, and in occupations that did not so readily welcome women, like law, theology, computers, and politics. Most of the mothers in academia have doctorates and ply their trades as teachers and researchers or have ascended the ladder of academic administration. Other mothers are artists, writers, psychotherapists, or paid community activists in feminist or public organizations. For some mothers, wage work was destiny, because they were not white or middle-class. But a career was rarely part of any mother's conscious expectations.

The mothers were not born to expect careers, nor were they born calling themselves feminists. That is how they can be captured in snapshots as postures frozen in time, words, perception. But that is not the way the daughters know them. The words that mothers used to convey their evolving feminist vision to their daughters were extremely important. More important was how the mother's consciousness, in the course of its own development, was expressed in daily life. The mothers' struggle to shake off the dust of tradition was the basic dynamic of the daughters' formative years.

The mothers attended school or went to work, arranged and rearranged daily life to fit changing circumstances; they negotiated with husbands or divorced them, reared their children alone for some years before another marriage, or consistently as single parents, and sometimes did some or all of the above in lesbian relationships.

They were denied jobs because certain work was considered inappropriate for women or because they had or might have children; they lost jobs because they were too outspoken about their feminism. They always changed their vocabularies and sometimes their appearance. They evaluated and reevaluated their goals and altered their lives accordingly—as feminists.

My friend Maxine once asked me whether many of the mothers, apart from their feminism, were conventional. In fact, there is no "apart from their feminism," and no matter how ordinary their lives seem from the outside to the casual observer, no matter how they complied with external norms of appearance, speech, or sexual and social convention, their feminism was a profound defiance of convention. The daughters as well know that growing up with a feminist mother created for them an extraordinary childhood. Sometimes it was exhilarating and fun, experienced as a privilege, as a righteous way to be. It could also be embarrassing—even painful—especially for the daughters who grew up in communities that disapproved of uppity women. Often the fun and the pain teetered in a delicate balance between the solidarity and support of the mother's feminist community and the disapproval of the larger community. Flying in the face of tradition, feminist mothers expected their daughters to do the same; daughters of feminists were sometimes bewildered and burdened by heavier parental expectations than their girlfriends or even their own brothers had. These expectations were also a source of strength and optimism.

Half of the daughters I interviewed grew up in families that appear to be "conventional" in structure and composition. I include under that irritating label families with both biological parents present, families in which the mother divorced and remarried while the daughter was young enough to consider the stepfather a parent, as well as families in which divorce occurred so late in the daughter's life that a stepfather, if he materialized, was irrelevant to her upbringing. In other words, we will begin by examining feminist families with mama, papa, and kids under one roof.

Adrienne's mother married at twenty-two and had two children by the time she was twenty-four. Until Adrienne was fourteen the family lived in a conservative Catholic neighborhood in a city on the East Coast. Her mother "was a product of the fifties and just tried to conform," or so her behavior would suggest. Adrienne, however, was aware from earliest childhood that her mother was doing what Carolyn Heilbrun describes as "writing her own life in advance of living it, unconsciously, and without recognizing or naming the process." In Adrienne's words, "I was always aware that she was very unhappy with her life, that staying at home and not working made her miserable." In the late sixties, when Adrienne was ten, her mother returned to university for a degree in social work. Four years later the family moved to the San Francisco Bay Area and the mother's career flourished in tandem with literary pursuits and feminist activities. The father was a character in the mother's evolving narrative by default: "As long as things ran, he didn't care what she did." Adrienne remembers her mother incessantly "asking, begging, pleading, fighting" for his help with the household chores. "But his job came first. He didn't want to deal with things. If the household was functioning, if she was not making too many demands on him, whatever she did was fine."

All the mothers, of course, tried to elicit their husbands' affirmation, or at least their cooperation, in reordering their domestic lives along more egalitarian lines. The point at which the family swerved from the main road to this unexplored byway influenced how bumpy the ride would be. Adrienne's mother was in her middle thirties and married for eleven years when she began consciously to write her life.

I interviewed four of the five Atkins daughters in upstate New York; Cary, Mia, Liza, and Antonia. Their mother, now an established writer, is seven years younger than Adrienne's. She had five children in eight years. "Dad helped take care of us, but he didn't do anything else. Mom was very upset." Liza, now twenty-five, recalls "how dramatically our lives began to change when my mom got involved in the women's movement. Certain things weren't tolerable anymore. So we changed from this traditional family to something else. It took many years to figure it out. It just got more and more egalitarian." The Atkins sisters observed and participated in this laborious transformation, as the father, a university professor, learned to accept his wife's quest for personal and professional fulfillment as equal to his. It required both parents to relinquish optimum professional achievement for the sake of an egalitarian family arrangement.

The Koenig sisters, Shanna and Rita, entered the world at an auspicious moment. Their mother, twelve years younger than Adrienne's, married when women already had a clear alternative to a life of quiet desperation. The family began its collective life guided by the mother's commitment to feminism and the father's commitment to egalitarianism. The Koenig sisters cannot remember a time when both parents did not share domestic chores.

Fairy tales with happy endings? Hardly. Bargaining and negotiating, cultivating respect for the mother's endeavors and weeding the soil of daily domestic obligations was a chronic feature of all the daughters' formative years. Even parents with the best intentions, like the Koenigs, could not always find a way around dilemmas posed by the facts of life in our times.

The Koenig daughters describe their father as their mother's best friend and ally in her feminist quest. He has educated himself in the history of women, he reads feminist literature, sees feminist films, understands the feminist perspective. Further, Rita points out that her father "recognizes that women's battles must be fought by women, that his mission is to educate other men." But as the elder of the Koenig sisters, Rita knows that the skewed relationship of male to female earnings affected her parents' roles at home. Her father is a physician; her mother became a nurse and a pioneer in midwifery. Rita knows that her father submits to professional demands on his time in order to pay the bills, because her mother's earnings cannot. Although the mother's work was as absorbing and demanding as her husband's, in the end it was she who did most of the child rearing.

Although a feminist husband and father is not an insurance policy against divorce, most of the marriages that survived the mothers' evolution did so because the husbands/fathers were prepared to and capable of accepting unanticipated responsibilities, of being more obliging or comradely than Adrienne's father. Renata's memories of her parents' marriage consist in large part of "lots of battles" over household chores, battles with questionable outcomes. When her father finally agreed to do the laundry, "he threw all of my mom's sweaters into the washing machine and shrunk them." Renata cannot suppress a giggle at the recollection—now. Perhaps her mother can laugh about it now, too. Renata's parents divorced when she was thirteen because her mother "realized that she wasn't the same person she had been when she fell in love with my father. He resented and sabotaged her ambitions, her goals—and her success. It wore her down, the furious battling over sharing duties."

To speak of outcomes, of course, is misleading. The daughters' adulthood does not mark the end of the mothers' journey, and mothers continue to reassess the past, to change in the present, and to imagine the future. The daughters remain their mothers' traveling companions. From her late adolescence, Shanna Koenig, now twenty, has been aware that her mother's life is still in flux: "In the last few years she's realized a lot about herself and about their marriage." Shanna's mother, for example, regretfully ponders what she might have done differently: "She went from her parents' house to a dorm to living with my father." In the light of her development over the years "there's definitely a difference now in how she sees her relationship with my father." As her mother questions aloud, Shanna remembers that in family quarrels her mother would get "emotional and upset—that was considered bad—and my father would be cool and logical—that was considered good." United though the parents were and are on important feminist issues, mother and daughter together delve deeper into what they call "traditional male/female power plays in the marriage."

Jennifer, too, remains a companion on her mother's ongoing pilgrimage. "My father is a really loving person and enjoyed us kids very much. But I know that one of my mom's great frustrations was that he didn't give her the help she needed. I never did understand why she didn't just say, 'George, for once let's do it my way.' She's only just beginning to be able to express these things to my father." Jennifer, like Shanna, learns from accompanying her mother into the present that there is more to an egalitarian relationship than who does the dishes.

Feminist mothers were often able to establish a degree of equality among their children that they could not always manage between themselves and their husbands. Holly's mother came to her marriage with a master's degree in public administration and today is county commissioner of social services. She worked throughout her children's childhood. When her mother was "really stressed out" her father would ask whether he could help. "But"—and here Holly fumbles in her otherwise smooth narrative—"he wasn't, well, he didn't do it automatically." Holly's mother *needed* her children's help. "I know that my mother was thrilled when we got older and could help in the house."

In a kind of atavism unexpected in late-twentieth-century urban households, children of feminist mothers became an economic asset. But feminist principle dictated how to allocate tasks. Where there were brothers the boys as well as the girls cooked, cleaned, laundered; Heather, proud and amused, reports that "my brother is one of the few boys I know who was capable of doing his own laundry when he moved out of the house." Not a single daughter complained that she and not her brothers was required to do the "women's" chores. Ironically, the easiest part was bringing boys into the woman's domestic sphere because, after all, it was feminist mothers who initiated and orchestrated the process of redefining gender roles.

But old thinking dies hard. Both before and after conventional feminist families began the process of transfor-

mation, fathers did the "men's" things; they tinkered
with the car, mowed the lawn and took out the garbage,
built the bookcases, and replaced the fuses. They did not
reveal the mysteries of "men's" work to their daughters.
Debby tells a typical story about a mother who "still buys
into it. She's still dependent on my father in certain ways:
'Sam, will you fix that, Sam, will you call the plumber,'
that kind of stuff." It did not change for the parents and
was passed down intact to the children. "My brothers
somehow acquired skills," Debby grumbles, "like fixing
toilets and building things. They helped my father and I
didn't. So now I have no instincts for these mechanical
skills. They come easily to my brothers. I resent it . . . I
should have done it too."

In other words, domestic chores aside, both parents in
conventional feminist families perpetuated many stereo-
typed gender skills and tastes. For obvious reasons, mothers rarely had their husbands' skills with machinery and
tools and did not wish to add them to their share of
housework. Fathers did what came "naturally" and
passed their skills to their male children. Grandmas,
grandpas, aunts, and uncles were complicit as well. Judith, who has an older sister and a younger brother,
recounts her family's saga of transition—and its flaws:

> Both parents took care of us. When I turned eleven,
> my father's schedule was more flexible than my
> mother's, so from that time he was home for us after
> school. He learned to iron and scrub and cook. We
> kids all learned to cook as well. There was no dif-
> ference in our domestic roles. But my sister and I
> were always aware that we were different from my
> brother. My brother was the only grandson on both

sides, so he always got the male toys, like trains. My sister and I got toys that we were supposed to share, female things. That really bothered us.

In Jennifer's experience, "there was not so much difference in my nuclear family. But in my extended family, boys were valued more than girls and given more leeway and attention. Like playing football was respected more than winning a spelling bee or sewing a dress."

Budding sexual behavior turns up repeatedly as an example of how brothers were favored. In a time of increasing sexual permissiveness for women, the freer hand that remained extended to the boys and withheld from the girls still irritates the daughters, even as they laugh about it in retrospect. When to date, whom to date, how late to stay out at night, whether to spend the night at the boyfriend's house or to have him in her room—"personal liberation" as Susanna puts it—was a powerfully contentious issue that often distinguished the boys from the girls. True, Susanna's parents expected the boys and the girls to develop and achieve equally, and family resources, economic and emotional, were allocated to them equally. But "on sexual issues, oh God, there was an incredible double standard in my family." Susanna remembers that her three brothers "were allowed to do everything and I was allowed to do nothing. The community honored my parents as a progressive couple, but I was dealing with their hypocrisy every day. I mean, if you're going to have a double standard for your boys and girls, you should confess it. Or vote for Phyllis Schlafly. The contradiction really made me furious."

Feminist families had a lot on their plates and some things just fell by the wayside. A feminist friend of mine once brought her six-year-old boy to play with my six-year-old girl. Scrutinizing my daughter's room, she sniffed superciliously; "Hmm. Some feminist you are! Evie has nothing for my son to play with." It was true. My daughter was not big on Barbie dolls, but she didn't care much for trucks either. On the other hand, that little son of a feminist looked down his nose at Evie's Raggedy Ann and her coloring books. Neither my friend nor I was always able to wriggle out of old ways of thinking. Both of us were single mothers. We did not have time or energy to attend to every detail of feminist parenting.

But there was one job we both undertook and never swerved from. In all the feminist families, fathers no less than mothers exhorted and encouraged their daughters, in word and deed, to develop their minds and to strive for and expect professional achievement. The daughters speak with one voice about how their parents instilled and nurtured their self-esteem, reminded them of their worth as women, affirmed their equality with men in ability, strength, and rights (at least in principle), and encouraged them to become self-sufficient. This is the strongest common denominator in the daughters' formative years.

In a curious twist to the distinctions that feminist families made between their male and female children, some daughters squirmed under a heavier weight of expectation. Throughout her childhood and adolescence, Linda felt that "*more* achievement was expected of me than of my brother. My brother could afford to be lackadaisical, because he wouldn't have to prove himself as I would. My mother had a sign over her desk that women have to work twice as hard to get half the recognition. I resented it, but I knew it was true. It *is* true."

Often mothers were quicker than fathers to temper optimism with caution. "Quite frankly, it was more my father who made me feel like I could do anything I wanted to." Adrienne pauses, surprised at her own words. "My mother's attitude was kind of 'Well, I *hope* you can, I *wish* you can, but it's a pretty tough world out there,' whereas my father's attitude was 'So what if you're a girl, you can do anything you want.'" Perhaps it is easier for a father to be cavalier about the obstacles to women's achievement that mothers know about from experience. A somewhat more cynical interpretation is offered by Nancy Chodorow in her influential book *The Reproduction of Mothering*: ". . . the young girl (and the woman she becomes) is willing to deny her father's limitations . . . as long as she feels loved."

But the daughters are very clear about their fathers' limitations. In the same measure that Adrienne's father encouraged her, he denied her mother; Adrienne judges her father harshly for making her mother's life more difficult than it had to be. She and the other daughters are expressing sober acknowledgment that fathers, no less than mothers, have to refashion their mentalities. Brenda evaluates her family for me: "I'm very proud of what my mother's accomplished. I'm proud of my father, too. Given his traditional upbringing, I'm sure he never imagined he'd have to cook meals and do that kind of child-rearing stuff. Sometimes he did it grudgingly, but he did it. So I've never doubted my right to an equal relationship. It never even crosses my mind that a man would expect me to do all the cooking and cleaning."

It may also be true, in Carolyn Heilbrun's words, "that it is through their daughters, rather than through their wives, that men first begin to question the powers of the patriarchy." I would amend that observation. The fathers begin to question the powers of the patriarchy because feminist wives pose the questions, stimulate and prod the fathers into discomfort or guilt. But it is often through their daughters that men can move from questions to answers, from thinking to behaving. Adrienne's father turned down a part in his wife's feminist scenario; his only contribution to Adrienne's mother was not to call off the whole show. But something must have been happening offstage, for what he could not give to his wife, he gave to his daughter. Brenda's father played his part in the egalitarian marital scenario grudgingly, but encouraged his daughter unstintingly. To emphasize the catalytic influence of a feminist mother does not belittle the father's achievement.

The other half of the daughters I interviewed did not grow up in conventional families. Feminist families without fathers are a kaleidoscope of living situations. There are daughters who cannot remember anything but a mother in the house; daughters who were old enough to remember the change from living with two parents to living with one; daughters who experienced yet another change if the mother remarried. For some the father-daughter relationship completely atrophied. In other cases the fathers remained a significant if attenuated influence. A few daughters shuttled between parents for varying periods of time, and a few grew up in communes. The experience that binds these histories is a life that for the most part was not shared with a father, a life managed by a feminist mother on her own. I am calling these families "mother families."

Simone de Beauvoir observed that for a girl, "the relative rank, the hierarchy, of the sexes is first brought to her attention in family life; little by little she realizes that if the father's authority is not that which is most often felt in daily affairs, it is actually supreme." To whatever degree paternal authority took center stage or hovered behind the scenes in feminist families with fathers in residence, it was obviously not an issue in the daily life of mother families, nor was the chronic bartering and negotiating over duties, obligations, and rewards. In the mother families, there was no husband to rely on for "men's" work, no "Sam, would you fix this; Sam, would you call the plumber." Egalitarianism became simply a process of parceling out what had to be done to whoever was around.

Lola's story is a kind of prototype. Lola, twenty-seven, is an African American daughter. Her mother (one of the first African American women to attend Yale nursing school in the early 1950s) interrupted her career for five years to stay home with her two daughters "because," says Lola, "my father insisted on it." For the next five years she worked as a Head Start school nurse so she could be home with her girls after school. When Lola was ten her parents divorced, and her mother, still working full time, went back to school full time as well to become a nurse practitioner. Lola and her sister routinely did what she called in her childhood "the boys' jobs," initially under protest, ultimately as a matter of course. "My mother refused to call in the boy next door, for example, to climb up on the roof and cover the air-conditioner. She just took it for granted that we could do it." And she marched her daughters off to karate classes, "all three of us—it was a pretty clear message. 'Ain't no man around, honey, let's go get ourselves some self-defense.' "

Marcia's father virtually disappeared from her life when she was an infant, and she grew up with her mother and grandmother. "Until I was fifteen or sixteen I didn't even know there was such a thing as boys' chores and girls' chores. I just did them all."

The daughters of mother families are convinced that they not only did different things, but also did more of everything in the household than the children of conventional feminist families. Perhaps so. We cannot do comparative time and motion studies of what happened in the past. Pride in their contribution to daily life is sometimes tinged with resentment—too much baby-sitting for younger siblings, too much cooking too early. Adulthood has transformed resentment into compassion. Emily speaks for many of the daughters of mother families: "I'm sure we did more than other kids, but my mother had such a hard time being a single parent. Now I respect my mother for making us do so many chores. She wanted us to learn to take care of ourselves. That's what a parent should do."

Feminist mothers were as vulnerable to the economic consequences of divorce as all divorced women: the father's income went up, the mother's went down. To be sure, the daughters of conventional families occasionally report a waxing and waning of family resources. What was scribbled in the margins of the stories of conventional families was written in bold type on every page of the mother families' stories: memories of living on food stamps and welfare, or of mothers' unrelenting conflicts with fathers over child support, of used clothing, of the mother who could not afford a car "so she rode a bicycle—in the suburbs yet, where that's considered really weird."

For the most part, the daughters took it in their stride and simply accepted being "poor" as a fact of life. They also knew that they lived better than many families. Their clothing may have been secondhand, but they were decently clothed. Their houses or apartments may not have been as fine as other children's, but they were adequately housed. The mothers' feminist values buoyed the struggle for economic survival with hope and optimism. The struggle for professional achievement, after all, was not simply a means to bigger and better consumption and acquisition. A vision of autonomy and fulfillment sustained the mothers—and their children—through the hardships of putting food on the table.

Still, I must confess that I was astonished (and uplifted) at the absence of childhood yearning for affluence. Renata says her mother "had to squeeze every little penny of child support out of my father. We really struggled. It takes more to feed and shelter a horse than what he gave us." She recalls that "we were maybe a step above welfare-and-food-stamp poor. I went to schools with middle- and upper-middle-class girls, and I do remember thinking, Oh, their houses are so nice. Little things like that." But Renata's childhood was enriched by her mother's feminist values and by the feminist community in which the family was embedded. "So," she continues, "economically we were poor, but in education, in values, in friends—no, we were definitely not poor. We were rich."

Today, the mothers are at a considerable remove from their early struggles. Some are extremely comfortable, some have modest incomes that still require counting, if not the pennies, certainly the dollars. None are poor, by any definition. The mother who began as a factory worker and is today a social worker doesn't enjoy the same affluence, status, and security as the mother who was once a struggling graduate student and is today a successful lawyer. But both—and all the mothers in between—are self-sufficient and successful by their own lights. The struggles, the successes, and the costs are indelibly imprinted on the daughters' consciousness.

Our culture squints at divorce statistics through an astigmatic blur. Somehow the collective consciousness has managed to blot out the varieties of household arrangements that have long been common among working-class families and some ethnic and racial minorities. Divorced and single-parent families menace the mythical norm; the nuclear family remains the way it's supposed to be. I wondered, after all is said and done, whether the daughters of mother families felt deprived or aberrant growing up without a father in the household. For even in communities where mother families were numerous and acceptable, where the feminist community challenged the nuclear family as the sole repository of social virtue and normality, the daughters read Dick and Jane books in school and watched "The Brady Bunch" on television.

Most of the daughters who never lived under one roof with a father did not regard their family arrangements as aberrations. Ellie, whose parents divorced when she was a year old, is entirely matter-of-fact about it; "It always seemed natural to me. When I got older and made friends with other people I thought it was strange to have two parents." Marcia's parents separated when she was an infant and she was reared by her mother and grandmother. "Most of the time it was pretty nice," she says. She mentions that her best friend wants a different kind of life than she does, a more "conventional" life. Marcia attributes the difference in their goals to the fact that "my friend's parents are together, a more normal family."

"Are you saying that a single-parent family isn't normal?" I ask.

"No, I wouldn't say that at all. It's normal. And I'm normal. It's just that I had a *different* experience. I wasn't raised to go to a father for this and a mother for that. There are differences between my family and hers, but I don't feel like I was cheated or missed anything. I got a good life, good values."

The experience of divorce and transition to a mother family was qualified by the moment in the daughters' young lives at which divorce occurred, how it was handled by the parents, whether and how the father remained present in their lives—all the considerations that one would expect in divorces of any families. At one extreme, Lola says that when her father left the house "it was as if we'd always lived in a dark tomb and someone had suddenly opened the windows. To be frank, it was very wonderful." At the other extreme are daughters whom the divorce left shattered and scarred. Luz was away at camp when her mother decided to leave her father. "At the end of the summer she picked me up at camp and told me in the car as we were driving home. It was really a trauma, a shock. It took a lot out of me. Now I understand where she was coming from. I like my father, but I sure wouldn't want to be married to him. But then I channeled all my anger at my mom. I hated her all through my adolescence."

Between the extremes is every reaction imaginable. One thing is clear: the daughters whose mothers drew them into a strong feminist community weathered the transition best. Linda was nine years old when her parents divorced, and she is still sorrowful about their separation. Now twenty-six and married, Linda is rethinking her childhood impression that her parents divorced because they both valued their careers above their family. She understands that it was far more complicated. The pain of that early life transition, however, was mitigated by her mother's feminist circle. "I would hang out with her and her feminist friends. I was everyone's daughter. It was a wonderful experience, because I could listen to them and learn from them as well as from my mother." Renata had a similar painful transition after her parents divorced when she was thirteen. But "all my mother's friends were feminists. I wouldn't call them my mothers, but I love them in that way. And I know they care about me in the same way." Such jubilant memories tumble forth from the daughters—of attending concerts of women's music and poetry readings, of exhibits of women's art, of feminist political meetings—and of being part of a community of women that sustained and succored. The daughters whose mothers, married or single, had cohesive feminist communities reflect back on those days with a kind of poignant nostalgia. Many of the daughters have not been able to replicate those bonds. Their mothers' feminist communities represent to them the halcyon days. "My mom and her friends, they had such wonderful relationships. They were so powerful, so beautiful. I wanted to *be* them!"

*　　*　　*

Imbedded in the national obsession with the nuclear family is the belief that children reared without a mother on duty twenty-four hours a day are cheated at best, downright deprived at worst. Remember—*all* the mothers, coupled and single, had been involved in serious, demanding endeavors outside the home, the majority from the daughters' earliest recollections. With this in mind I ask the daughters, whatever the composition of their families, whether they had felt neglected while they were growing up.

Only two daughters, Luz and Cynthia, meet the culture's dreariest expectations—almost. Their stories are remarkably similar. Luz's mother, a factory worker with no higher education, began taking college courses when Luz was three years old—one course at a time because "that was all she could afford, and all she could manage with two small kids, a full-time job, and my father, who came home from work, sat down in a chair with his poodle, and watched television." Soon after the divorce the mother completed her graduate training as a social worker. The father did not contribute to the family's support.

> She used to come home so stressed out that I couldn't talk to her. A kiss good-night, hello in the morning. I must have felt neglected, because I was so violent. It was a way of calling attention to myself. Hey, look at me! I'm beating up my sister again, or kicking the dog.

Luz had three troubled years in late adolescence replete with drugs, alcohol, and "terrible, abusive relationships with guys." After high school, two more years of the same: "I was lost. I had no idea what to do, no desire to do anything." Now, at twenty-three, Luz is finishing her second year of college. She is involved with a young man whom she describes as a feminist.

"What turned you around?" I ask her.

"My mom had a lot of influence on me. When I was growing up *we never talked*." Luz pounds the table in rhythm with her words. "She didn't have room in her head for me. But now we talk about everything. And now I realize that the independence I learned as a kid was good. It took a lot of pain and heartache to appreciate that, but in the end I can make my own choices and take care of myself."

Cynthia's mother is a paid community activist and a founder of her community's Hispanic Women's Association. Like Luz's mother, she worked in a factory by day, went to school at night, and cared for three small children and a husband. She left Cynthia's father when Cynthia was ten.

Cynthia dropped out of high school at fourteen and ran away from home. "My mom was going to school at night, trying to make herself better and trying to make life better for us," she says. "I knew she was doing her best, but I never heard her say, 'I love you and I want to be with you, but I can't. I'm doing this for all of us.' " A year later Cynthia married a man—a boy, really—who was "possessive, jealous, and demanding, just like his father." She stayed with him for four years: "Four years of misery may not seem so long, but for me it seemed like a lifetime." Now, with a two-year-old child and a divorce, Cynthia works part time and attends a community college that accepts students without high school degrees.

In Luz's house and in Cynthia's house there was always an adult around to take care of the children's physical needs and some of their emotional needs. An adored and doting aunt lived with each family intermittently for long periods, and baby-sitters took over in the intervals. Physical neglect is not the issue, and was not for any of the daughters. Luz and Cynthia are talking about emotional neglect. As the mothers, both Latinas, struggled to feed their families and simultaneously to create a new destiny for themselves, sometimes important things fell through the cracks.

Luz's and Cynthia's stories are atypical in their extremity. The other daughters who express a sense of neglect present a less stark, more subtle picture. "I was never a latchkey kid," Anne-Marie says. The varieties of child-care arrangements in her young life included a stint in a commune, which she liked the best. "But sure, I felt neglected. I'm proud that my mother went to school and I knew that it was an economic necessity for her to work. But there were periods when I didn't get the emotional sustenance that I needed."

Rachel, the eldest of two daughters, speaks of her family as a model she would like to emulate. "I definitely felt neglected at times," she says. Her mother "would concentrate so hard on her work or her reading that there was no room for me. But I felt very loved, and if I really needed her she was there."

The daughters' needs and perceptions fluctuated with the stages in their lives and in balance with their mothers' lives. Nor were the daughters simply the passive receivers of what life threw at them. Susanna "felt fine" until she was thirteen. "At that point I began to feel neglected. So I just went with her all the time to meetings and demonstrations or whatever. It was my choice to do that, to be close to her."

I ask Adrienne whether she felt abandoned or neglected when her mother threw herself first into school and then work. "God, no. I was happy. Before, she was so miserable that she made enormous emotional demands on us. When she went to school and to work it was like she finally had something of her own, and it gave me a lot more freedom. It was a relief."

In fact, the great majority of daughters greet my question about feeling neglected with raised eyebrows. Why would I ask such a question? The cookies-and-milk paradigm, which they often bring up spontaneously, makes them laugh. "You know, there's a lot in it for the kids, too. I learned to be independent. When I went to friends' houses and their mothers were ready with the cookies and milk, I never pined for that," Becky says, articulating a variation on the common theme. "I wouldn't have had it any other way. I'm glad she was involved in other things besides the family. It helped me to work out what is important in life. I got the good part of it." The good part was independence. The good part was being drawn into their mothers' activities, feminist and otherwise: "Sure I felt a bit neglected now and then, with child care and all. But she took me with her to a lot of things, to school, to work, to meetings, to parties. So it went both ways." The good part was respect for their mothers' struggles and successes, and respect for their mothers' loving, if not perfectly successful, efforts to care for them.

Every community provided its own growing medium for feminism and feminists. Some were rich and nourishing, others were meager and barely sustaining. If, for example, I had chosen to interview daughters only from the San Francisco Bay Area, the picture would be significantly skewed. During the daughters' childhood and adolescence the San Francisco ethos tolerated, indeed encouraged, experimentation and defiance of tradition. The political atmosphere was especially engaged and expressive. It still is even today as gourmet food and good living compete for attention with political and social issues. Among the California mothers in my sample there is more divorce and remarriage and more interracial marriage than in other communities. There are more single mothers and more mothers, married and single, who reconnoitered the terrain of unconventional living arrangements such as communes. And although these mothers were not entirely free of community antagonism to feminism and to feminists, they found less of it. To be sure, feminist enclaves also emerged and survived in more conservative areas, and families of all types were politically engaged, exposing the daughters to a range of concerns typical of the period. I do not wish to imply that the atmosphere of the community, any community, affected the daughters uniformly and predictably. But the community certainly influenced each daughter's formative years, regardless of her own family's composition.

The Atkins daughters were born in Washington, D.C. In their earliest recollections the family living room bustles with people who envelop the young girls in feminist and other political activities, in consciousness-raising discussions, and who accompany them on demonstrations and marches. When the Atkins family moved to a city in the Rust Belt, a troubling isolation replaced the vibrant community it had left behind. The family became a feminist oasis in a conservative community that regarded feminism with suspicion and antagonism. Like Mia, whom we met in the previous chapter, each of the Atkins sisters has a repertoire of tales of harassment and hostility that could fill a book. I hope they write that book someday. Now Liza laughs as she tells her stories, but they were not so funny then:

> In junior high school my math teacher told a joke at the beginning of the year: Ten German men jumped a girl in the alley; she said "nein, nein," so one of the men left. Then whenever the number nine came up, the teacher would say, "Nine, like the German girl in the alley." I went up to him and said, "That's a rape joke. It's not funny." I said it politely, smiling. The second time I protested he sent me down to the principal.

Liza's school days were punctuated by such incidents. "In the seventh grade I got the best grade in an Industrial Arts class. All the boys followed me around, chanting 'slut, slut, slut.' " This time the boys were sent down to the principal, but "from then on all the way through senior year the kids would say, 'Oh, you'd better watch out for Liza. She's this radical.' "

Cary, the youngest and "the last Atkins feminist," as she was called by schoolmates and teachers, was not surprised by teachers who "would say incredibly sexist things to get my goat." Nonetheless she was overwhelmed by an incident in her tenth-grade history class. "My history teacher assigned a paper on significant people, not including women—because, he insisted, women in the past didn't do anything significant except have babies and marry rich men. I chose George Sand." Cary dissolves in laughter. "I thought she was a man!" She laughs again as she recalls how the teacher "just blew up."

Nettled and defiant, Cary chose another historical personage—Christine de Pisan—and for her pains received a *D.* "The teacher screamed at me in front of the whole class that I hadn't proved she was significant. His argument was that he had a master's degree in history and he knew there were no significant women in history."

The incident exploded into a school scandal. Cary's parents wrote a letter of protest; her mother's colleagues at a writing colony read the paper and wrote additional letters; the school principal and the head of the history department read the paper and agreed that the grade was unfair. But Cary's history teacher prevailed and the *D* grade remained. In retrospect Cary regards the incident as "a great story. It made me stronger." The Atkins sisters regard their collective experience of community hostility as a trial by fire that forged in them strength and self-confidence, equipping them to face adult life.

Although all mothers do peculiar things in public that embarrass their young children, feminist mothers had their own special brand of idiosyncracies. Nicole remembers how her mother would bounce into PTA meetings "in overalls with paint splashed all over them."

> I'd say, "God, can't you wear a nice little skirt and a blouse?" And she'd say, "No, I am who I am." It was embarrassing then, but it was a good model for me. *I am who I am.* That comes back to me all the time.

Side by side with stories of the mothers' amusing escapades or less humorous but uplifting memories are tales of great and sometimes enduring pain. Amelia is from a large southwestern city. Her parents divorced when she was six months old and her sister three years old. Her mother, a feminist psychotherapist, did not remarry. From the start a single-parent family was a bit peculiar in this community. But worse:

> My mother was always out there mending a fence, building a deck, laying bricks in the garden, always with a hammer in her hand. There I was, twelve years old, hanging Sheetrock with my mother and my sister. People would come by and stare.

Today, like the Atkins daughters, Amelia cherishes her hard-won strength. Then, however, it was not just embarrassing or funny. "I always asked myself what the hell's the difference if it's a man or a woman with a hammer? But it was really hard. I was so different from everyone else."

Whatever the daughters feel now as young adults, a hostile community could be the source of early suffering. Melissa grew up in an affluent suburb of a middle-sized midwestern city. Her parents divorced when she was five. She does not lament the divorce. On the contrary, she respects her parents for making a decision that was healthy for both of them. "The first thing people say to me when I tell them that I'm from divorced parents is how sorry they are for me. I really don't understand what they mean. I never felt deprived. My parents were both always there for me."

However, after the divorce her mother, a teacher and journalist, created a world within a world that Melissa describes as a "hippie" enclave in an affluent middle-class suburb where "it was not the thing to do." Then, when Melissa was nine, her mother came out as a lesbian and four years later brought her lover into the family.

"I hated it. It was very difficult. They [the mother and her lover] were not out to flaunt it, but I *never* invited friends over. I was afraid of what other people would think." And she still is. Melissa is now at a university in the same community, and to this day she does not reveal her mother's lesbianism to friends and acquaintances. Not once in the three hours we spoke together could she bring herself to use the word *lesbian*. When I brought up feminism, she responded as if I had asked about lesbianism. When homosexuality was the topic, she talked about feminism. Neither, to the extent that Melissa can separate one from the other, is "the accepted thing in society today. It's not something people consider normal."

By contrast, the daughters of lesbian feminist mothers in the San Francisco Bay Area regard their mothers' homosexuality with equanimity. When Judith's mother left her husband for a woman it disrupted the family, but "living in San Francisco made it easy." Judith grins. "It was almost a status symbol. When I told friends my mother was a lesbian, they'd say, 'Oh, that's cool,' or 'How interesting,' or 'Do you know so-and-so, her mother's a lesbian too.' It helped me to figure out what I think about homosexuality."

Facing up to community hostility in the San Francisco Bay Area was easier in many ways. The Koenig family's experience is one example. The mother is African American, the father Caucasian; the daughters spent their earliest years in a self-sustaining rural commune that they still visit regularly, although it is now only a fragment of what it was twenty years ago. The commune has taken on a mythic quality that illuminates their lives. After they left the commune for the city, the Koenig household consistently spilled over the boundaries of its nuclear core. A shifting cast of aunts, cousins, friends, and other families shared the Koenigs' premises and their concerns with feminism, civil rights, and antiwar activities. Shanna Koenig ran with a pack of daughters of feminists whose favorite epithet for teachers, male and female, was "male chauvinist pig." Confronting them was sport—but serious sport. In the seventh grade the girls mounted a campaign against the prevailing dress code: "Girls couldn't wear shorts to school, but boys could wear whatever they damn well pleased." The tactics were simple: "All the girls showed up to school in shorts on a certain day. We were all sent home." But the dress code was changed.

Still, Shanna and her friends understood that even in Berkeley they were members of a subculture. The town, their schools, were full of "straight" girls from "traditional" families, where the fathers worked and the mothers stayed at home ready with—what else?—milk and cookies after school. Those girls were "preppies," and if heads were counted they probably outnumbered Shanna's crowd. But in this community it was Shanna and company whose values prevailed.

In more conservative communities as well, the daughters of feminists sought out one another. If they were not as sassy or assertive as the Koenig sisters, they nonetheless drew strength and affirmation from their collective identity. In Renata's midwestern high school "there was this really huge group of kids, the conforming preppies. The worst thing about them was that they were so shallow and fickle. I don't know, maybe some of them had good friends. But my friends, we were *really* friends. And creative, interesting girls as well."

Community is more, much more, than a physical space shared by people who have only proximity in common. Even in the most homogeneous communities subtle gradations of opinion, attitudes, expectations, and values bump up against each other in complex and powerful ways, positive and negative. Certainly the community's influence on the daughters of feminists eludes tidy, definitive conclusions. The Atkins family, large and cohesive, was its own feminist community within a larger community that was hostile to almost everything the family valued. The five Atkins daughters paid dearly in childhood, but today they echo Mia with gusto: "I loved growing up in this family, this wonderfully strange, very different kind of family." Amelia, growing up in an isolated feminist family surrounded by a hostile community, wonders whether "every daughter of a feminist has experienced my struggles, has hurt the way I did. It's good for me now, but it wasn't good for me then." Clearly, a feminist childhood was easier when it was not necessary to scratch around for confirmation.

But people who do not inhabit a cohesive physical space can comprise a community of ideas, emotions, perspectives, and goals. They reach each other through books, read about one another in the newspapers, hear each other speak in public or talk to each other on the telephone. As Antonia says, "The minute I read a book that has nonsexist language, I have this amazing, overwhelming feeling of being included. I don't feel alone." That is the kind of community that feminist mothers had and provided for their daughters, even when the immediate geographical community made life difficult. That is what strong women who do not call themselves feminists did not have in the past and do not have now. It is a community of consciousness that allows its members to "do incredible things," not in isolation and *in spite of* being a woman—but *because* they are women in concert with other women, wherever they may be.

CHAPTER THREE

The Fantasy

*Responsibility to yourself . . . means that you refuse
to sell your talents and aspirations short, simply to
avoid conflict and confrontation. And this, in
turn, means resisting the forces in society which say
that women should be nice, play safe, have low
professional expectations, drown in love and forget
about work, live through others, and stay in the
places assigned to us.*

—ADRIENNE RICH, *ON LIES, SECRETS,
AND SILENCE,* 1979

"What is your best fantasy?" I
ask the daughters of feminists, suggesting they project
five, ten, twenty years into the future. I expect them to
begin with imaginative excursions into exotic places of
the planet, of the mind and heart, of the purse. Then, I
anticipate, we will slowly make our way back to real life.
I hope to encourage them to explore how they perceive
themselves as women in their time. They do—but not as
I expected. Real life is very much on their minds. Their
definitions of real life, however, would have been unimaginable for their mothers at that age.

My own dreams about my adult future must have begun around the age of eight. A child of the city streets, I longed for country pleasures. In those days if you wanted nature, you married someone who could give it to you, right? I decided I would have to marry a farmer. An occasional subversive thought flickered in my consciousness. Maybe I could be a forest ranger and enjoy nature in romantic solitude from the top of a fire tower deep in the forest. I squelched this: To be a forest ranger was, like the title of one of my favorite mysteries, "an unsuitable job for a woman." As words and language nudged nature to the periphery, I thought about being a writer. Ah, that's better. That's something I could do as a wife and mother. But even that concession to the primacy of wifehood and motherhood was insufficient, and by the time I was in high school, I knew enough to keep my mouth shut. When my high school rhetoric teacher assigned the class a speech about our "ambitions," I dutifully recited the party line: a modest job until I married and had children and then devotion to them and their father. I half believed it, really believed it, and I half suspected it might be nonsense. Lacking vocabulary and courage, in public I suppressed the nonsense and celebrated marriage as the mediator of my fate.

For the thirtieth reunion of my high school class, the organizers assembled an updated yearbook. Alongside our old photographs, earnest seventeen- and eighteen-year-olds in hilarious hairdos, were thirty years of autobiography crammed into a couple of paragraphs. I did my research and tabulated the results: my female classmates married between thirty seconds and three years after graduation, including the girl with the magnificent operatic voice, the ace athlete, and the (seemingly) archetypal bluestocking. Here is a model synopsis of how my old girlfriends write their lives in retrospect:

Mary Smith Jones. Married to Harold for twenty-nine years. Harold is a successful (lawyer-entre-preneur-accountant) who has won three awards for (fill in the blank) and travels frequently to international meetings. He has received awards from (Kiwanis-Jewish Federation-Catholic Charities). Three children: Sally, married with two children; Sharon, married, expecting her first child; Arthur (doctor-lawyer-computer programmer).

Of the sixty-six women who supplied biographies, six were divorced. If their daughters are doing something else besides planning to marry, my old pals aren't telling. Eleven women revealed active work lives that, with only a few exceptions, began after their children were grown and out of the house. I don't know what childish stories my classmates told themselves in the dark at bedtime. One Mary Smith Jones ended her autobiography this way: "I still want to be a neurosurgeon when I grow up." But in high school we did not discuss such things. We designed luscious wedding dresses, scrutinized our girl-friends for prospective bridesmaids, and doodled possible married names in the margins of our English composition notebooks—Mrs. His-First-Name-His-Surname.

I think the daughters of feminists would read my retrospective yearbook as archaeology rather than history. When I invite the daughters of feminists to dream about their futures, they immediately and invariably talk about work and career. Work, which for the mothers was a hard-won prize, is the daughters' birthright. These young women have imbibed from their mothers the absolute centrality of work: work as normal, necessary, fulfilling.

To say that work is central implies that everything else is peripheral, and some daughters mean exactly that. For most, however, work is necessary but not sufficient. Work is the first thing on their minds because it is the soil from which everything else will grow—marriage, motherhood, friendships, community, and social involvement.

The media drown us in images of women, suited and briefcased, marching resolutely into the corporate world, cheerily bowing to its demands, embracing its values, eager for its material rewards—and getting them. We are assured that this is the fulfillment of the feminist dream. True, not everyone loves the new cultural heroine. Some denounce her as a violation of nature's design for women and blame her for family disintegration, crime, juvenile delinquency, drug abuse, and the current problem of the week. The accusation, of course, is an ideological assumption, not a demonstrable conclusion. A better criticism would be that the image of Ms. Corporate America is a modern fairy tale as irrelevant to most women as Sleeping Beauty or Cinderella. In her book *On Her Own: Growing up in the Shadow of the American Dream,* Ruth Sidel interviewed young women of the daughters' generation and discovered that they too dream about work. Their heart's desire is to have glamorous, high-paying jobs that will allow them to "consume in an upper-middle-class manner." It does not matter what part of the country they come from, what their class, race, or ethnicity. They want it, and they are convinced they can get it. Sidel also demonstrates that the social and economic realities of this country deliver the goods only to very few. Young women have been duped, she concludes. They mistake stardust for reality.

The daughters of feminists have a different vision. Their dreams are not woven of tinsel and spangles, but of serviceable workaday materials whose snags and defects are part of the fabric, subject to unraveling and to mending as well. For all of that, the fantasy evokes adventure and exploration, and, like all true adventure, it is as much a journey of reversals as of progression. They begin their journey with eyes on the prize of self-reliance.

The daughters never question that they are responsible for their own economic survival. Prince Charming is dead, buried, and unmourned, at least as a provider. They simply do not trust men to support them. This refrain is regular and incessant. It is sung without rancor, only occasionally with cynicism, but always fiercely, tenaciously. It transcends family history and dreams of family in the future. It is prologue and epilogue to the fantasy.

This is hardly surprising in the daughters of mother families. "I remember thinking when I was a child that you've got to make sure you can take care of yourself *by* yourself, and your children as well," Lola recalls. The other daughters who were supported by mothers throughout childhood and adolescence echo her thought. "I could never depend on a man to support me. I don't intend to be flattened if he leaves me or dies. I never did have a man to depend on, so I can't even imagine what it's like," says another daughter of a mother family.

In conventional feminist families, however, the mothers were often fully supported by husbands in the daughters' early years, and have usually remained the junior contributor to the family coffers. But neither do these daughters expect to be supported. Shanna Koenig sees beyond her own stable family to the world around her: "I have lots of friends whose fathers deserted the family. My friends were raised by single mothers who don't have careers. Such struggle! I have to be self-sufficient. Definitely. I never want to depend on someone else financially. Not for myself, not for my children."

The daughters know all about women and poverty. Some have lived it, others have seen it with their own eyes. The daughters who took childhood hardship in their stride think about it differently now as they contemplate adulthood and especially motherhood. Ingrid lived on welfare while her mother attended university. After several communal living arrangements they moved into a house shared with another woman. Ingrid slept in an enclosed unheated porch: "When the food-stamp people came to inspect us, we had to put a stove and food and all the stuff from my room into my mother's room, so we could say we were living in one room. I wore clothes we scavenged from the free box." There is no melancholy in these recollections. Ingrid tells them like a series of amusing escapades that ended in triumph for her and her mother. It was fun for Ingrid the child, but not for Ingrid the prospective parent.

Even those who have learned about women and poverty from college courses or from television do not think of themselves as members of a charmed elite to whom such things could not happen. Rachel describes her parents, married for thirty years, as an exemplary feminist couple, stable, loving, and egalitarian. "When I think about having a family, they are definitely my model," she says. Some years ago Rachel collaborated on a documentary film about poverty and single mothers. The exposure to "women living on the edge was an intense experience," and Rachel is as frightened by the possibility that she could end up like them as she is reassured by her own family history. As the recession of the early 1990s deepened, the daughters' anxiety about economic survival deepened with it. They see poverty for what it is—frightening, degrading, and to be avoided.

Many feminist mothers, if they were middle-class, rebelled against the earnest getting and spending of their own parents, and they flirted, however briefly, with the romance of the "culture of poverty" in the sixties and seventies. But for the daughters, there is nothing "cool" about being poor. Ingrid explains, "I don't want to be scraping nickels and dimes together to buy diapers. There's enough stress in bringing up a child without worrying about money too." She is thinking, appropriately, about her own peace of mind as well as of a child's welfare. The daughters speak of decent housing in safe neighborhoods: "I want a roof over my head" is the common metaphor for survival, for security, colored perhaps by the enormity of homelessness today.

Survival and security, of course, are subjective, and one woman's survival is another woman's deprivation. Luz grew up poor, by anyone's definition. Her mother is no longer poor but she cannot afford to help Luz through college, so Luz works thirty hours a week, nights and weekends, to put herself through a full-time college program. Her professional goal to teach disadvantaged children in elementary school is hardly the road to big bucks. But by the time she's in her midthirties, she says with a mischievous smile, she wants a Mercedes. Red! Convertible! I think she's pulling my leg, but she isn't—not quite. "I don't care how old it is," she adds, "but I want it." The car is a symbol of what she hopes to have achieved by her own efforts.

Like Luz, the daughters are neither saints nor ascetics, but they have little appetite for lavish consumption. Survival and security are givens, high living is a game not worth the candle. Susan is thirty-four. After a decade on a self-sustaining commune she returned to the "real world" and spent "a few miserable years" as a real estate agent. Then she married, had two children who are now one and three, and returned to university to study early childhood development. Her husband is a graduate student in finance. We talk about the low salaries of nursery school teachers.

"If we were to split up, I'd be in the position that countless women are. I'd be teaching nursery school for six bucks an hour and he'd be making a fucking fortune."

"You're prepared to take that risk?"

"Yes. And it's a risk for any woman. But it's not as bad for my soul as making money in the corporate world. Going out and making money in the corporate world is not my definition of feminism."

Only one daughter says outright that her fantasy for ten years in the future is to have "a lot of money."

"For what purpose?" I ask.

"Freedom," she replies. "It gives you the freedom to do all the other things you want to do." She pauses, begins to speak, and pauses again. Something else is clearly at stake, and she has a hard time putting her thoughts together. When she does, she shifts her ground. "I think self-esteem and financial independence are tied to each other. When I feel financially dependent on my husband, I begin to put pressure on him because he's my sole support, my security. But if you make your own money you can pour energy into yourself, because you're the source of your own stability." Translated, freedom "to do all the other things you want to do" means making the money yourself. As another daughter put it, "One thing my mom drummed into my head is 'Have your own money. Make sure you never have to ask a man for money to buy a bra.' " According to the daughters, it is not healthy to be beholden to a husband who controls the purse.

The paycheck is a source of pride, the pride that comes from contributing, from fairness, from "carrying my own weight." The paycheck means adulthood. After Becky's parents divorced, her father married a woman who is the diametrical opposite of Becky's mother—a housewife. Becky has an affectionate relationship with her stepmother, but finds her an enigma. "It was always so weird to me, and it still is. You know, she gets her allowance from him—like she's still a little kid."

Half the women I interviewed are students, undergraduate or graduate. Among the other half some are purposefully working toward a lifelong career and others are still trying on hats. In this time of frenetic career building spurred by economic anxiety, I am surprised at how serenely many daughters take time to experiment. Judith is twenty-seven and in her second year of law school, but only after having been a baker, a janitor, an artist's model, and a community organizer. Amy, a corporate success, did one long stint as a congressional aide and another in a city planning department. Marcia is a deputy sheriff, working the night shift while she completes a degree in business administration. Nina, an environmental instructor, worked as a security guard at rock concerts. For Susan, a late entry to the university, full-time work was ten years in a "hippie commune." Amelia, a bartender, speaks for all: "I'm really sick of jobs. I want something that has meaning for me, something that grabs me."

The vocabulary of work is rich and complex and speaks

of far more than economic security. It is a vocabulary of self-esteem, challenge, absorption, creativity: "The idea of making a living doing something I love, something I feel *passionate* about, is the ultimate fantasy for me."

At twenty-eight Rachel uses her skills as a gardener and landscaper to build a thriving and satisfying business that fully supports her, her boyfriend, and his child. The boyfriend left paid employment for several years to renovate a house they bought together. Someday in the future, they reckoned, the boyfriend would go back to work and they would rent out rooms in the house to augment their joint incomes. Now they are separating, and Rachel is reevaluating her fantasy. Finding a provider is not part of it.

"Would you mind being supported, now that you have done it the other way around?" I ask.

"No way! Too much of my self-esteem comes from supporting myself."

Rachel loves being a woman in a traditionally male trade. "There are a lot of women in horticulture, but not many in hands-on landscaping and construction. So I run into a lot of sexism. But it doesn't upset me. It's a challenge, and I like being different."

"Different from what?" I ask.

"Different from people's expectations. When I do a good job, I like getting respect and acknowledgment because I know it wasn't quite what my customers expected. I enjoy the power of overseeing men, like the ones who do irrigation. It feels good."

In Ruth Sidel's sample of young women, the very few who were choosing the so-called caring professions "spoke mainly of their concern that these professions would pay enough to enable them to live the life-style they hoped for." But her dismal findings about the lack of social conscience among young women does not hold for the daughters of feminists. Some, of course, look inward, charting a course toward artistic careers as performers or painters. For most, however, personal fulfillment and doing good are indivisible.

We have met Lola in previous chapters. A twenty-eight-year-old African American, she has just received her master's degree in documentary film production. Her thesis film, shown on public television, has earned lavish accolades. Her best fantasy is to make four acclaimed films in the next five years.

"Can you imagine not working?" I ask.

Lola rolls her eyes. "It's as if you're asking me about breathing. It's like asking me if I anticipate needing air five years from now." She needs air, she needs work. She uses words like *independence, pride, power,* and she speaks of the economic climate. *And* she wants some of the material rewards. "I know this couple, they've been married for sixteen years. No children. They have a gorgeous apartment and a full-time housekeeper. They work, travel, and they have an amazingly loving, supportive relationship." But this is the gravy; the meat and potatoes is her mission. Lola's thesis film, a documentary about a black woman of extraordinary talent, courage, and achievement, is the first of many on her agenda: "Some little girl somewhere is flipping the dial and she sees sleek women in leotards doing push-ups and the ads for makeup and perfume, or women cooing over their clean laundry. Suddenly she sees this compelling black woman and—God!—she's a judge. I believe in the power of the media. What you see is what you become." Lola's mission is to offer alternatives to media stereotypes of women.

Jenna, twenty-one, studies biology to equip herself for

a career in environmental work. She has a powerful concern for environmental improvement. But it could be replaced by a passion to right other social wrongs, because the passion and the work are instrumental, a means to something else. "I want to make a difference, that's my fantasy, really making a difference and spending all my time doing it. I want to be heard, understood, respected." Making a lot of money is irrelevant; "I only want to earn enough to keep myself alive."

At twenty, Shanna Koenig is considering a career in politics, but she has lost interest in her third-grade ambition "to be the first black woman president." The difference between her childhood fantasy and my modest dream of being a forest ranger amazes me. To be heard, to make a difference in the world, to do good—most daughters want that. I am perplexed, however, by the absence of really wild fantasies, spectacular dreams. None of the daughters talk now about finding a cure for cancer, winning a Nobel prize for literature, or being president. It is enough to penetrate traditional male enclaves—industrial design, politics (professional politics, not volunteer work), filmmaking, police work. Like their fathers' and brothers' mechanical skills, mathematics, physics, and engineering still do not beckon. They are attracted to the "soft" sciences, like environmental studies and biology. The daughters who want academic careers are in the humanities.

Although only one daughter is a corporate success, many had a fling with corporate life, at least in the imagination, before they rejected it. "I thought a business degree would expand my horizons," Marcia says. "It hasn't. That corporate woman—it's not the woman I want to be." Renata, who thought about being a corporate lawyer, concludes that the rewards are as unattractive as the costs. Her roommate is the archetypal Ms. Corporate America. "She has tons of money. She blows two hundred dollars on a blouse. A blouse! Can you imagine?" She makes a sour face. "No, I don't find it glamorous at all. I find it horrifying." Renata is still casting about for a satisfying, fulfilling career. But she is firm about the push away from "the yuppie stuff. I don't want to be in a world where you have to please a bunch of creeps in what you say, what you wear, how you act."

Paradoxically, the daughters who have chosen the most traditional women's careers, elementary school teaching and nursing, do the most profound soul-searching. Pursuing a typical women's vocation requires them to rise above a certain taint and, in many cases, to resist parental promptings to follow a feminist script that deliberately rejects "women's work." When Amy's younger sister Beth enrolled in nursing school, their father was confused and upset: "Damn it, if you're going to put all that work into it, why don't you go to medical school and become a doctor?" Patiently, but with some exasperation, Beth would explain, "But, Dad, I don't *want* to be a doctor. I don't like doctors. I *want* to be a nurse." Actually, Beth got her nursing degree as a way to legitimize her true goal—midwifery—because she did not even want to work under a doctor. Dad is still scratching his head.

Debby is a bit surprised to find that she has become a teacher and more than a bit surprised to find that she loves her work: "Ten years ago I absolutely did not fantasize about being a teacher because, like many people, I put it down—a feminine profession." Christine, too, loves her work as an elementary school teacher. When she began college she scoffed at the prospect because "I was raised to believe I could be anything I wanted to be." Dreaming about "corporate stuff," she enrolled in a business major because "I wanted something more than a female stereotype." Corporate stuff turned out to be something less.

"Corporate work is selfish. I began to realize that I want to make a difference in the world and in people's lives. Some people think school teaching is easy because it's a typical woman's job. But you know, teaching is challenging. You have a lot of power, you're a manager, a social worker. You can really make a difference."

How do the daughters who teach elementary school feel about the low pay? The answer: To hell with it and with society's stereotypes. Debby sums it up: "Yes, the pay is low, but I get a lot of psychic income."

Whatever it is that the daughters of feminists seek—livelihood, independence, esteem, power, fulfillment, contribution—they believe they will get it directly through their own work. Work is their right and their obligation, the core of identity for many, and as important as the other facets of selfhood for those who think of it as only a part of the whole. To a woman they are conscious every day of their lives of their mothers' determination to blast open the doors of professional possibilities. They are grateful and optimistic.

At the beginning of this chapter I suggested that the daughters of feminists do not have heads full of glamorous fluff about their working futures, that their vision is sober and realistic. Do they also believe that there are no obstacles to their success, however they define it, as working women?

The daughters who have chosen traditional women's work, of course, are more comfortable day in and day out than those who have chosen traditionally male fields. Holly works in a municipal agency for the prevention of child abuse. The agency depends on the benevolence of municipal legislators, who are all men. She describes them as rude, crude, and dismissive of the agency's needs. "I don't know if it's because we're a human services agency or if it's because we're all women." (She hasn't quite figured out that human service agencies usually are "all women.") But everything is fine on a day-to-day level: "Our agency is all female. Of course we don't discriminate against each other."

Nina knows perfectly well that in her state-funded agency for environmental education all the teachers are women and all the administrators are men, but she doesn't mind: "We're out in the trenches and they're in the office. I didn't pick this work to sit in an office and shuffle papers."

In predominantly male fields the daughters do not find either the daily atmosphere or their prospects for the future so agreeable. The daughters in the legal profession, for example, confront obstacles at every stage of their careers. Law school, Judith explains, is still a man's game. The classes may be half female, but the faculty is mainly male. She has begun her career with few role models in the classroom, with sexist language from male instructors, and with a clear sense that to succeed in school and later as a lawyer she must conform to male definitions of professionalism: "Loyalty to a law firm means that you have to give them your life and a few other things." Is this an obstacle? Not exactly. Judith will avoid the big corporate law firms and work in public interest law, where she feels the standards and atmosphere are more congenial to women.

Amy, who painfully bumped her nose against the glass

ceiling at her corporate trading company, was denied promotion "not for lack of accomplishment, but for my style of management. And I wasn't one of the boys. They couldn't talk to me about sports and stuff." She quit and found a new job. Some time after our original interview, Amy told me that her new job has not been much of an improvement. She'll keep looking.

Anne-Marie has worked in computers and administration for six years and now supervises a department of seven people. She still has to remind people that she is not a secretary, and she is repeatedly passed over for promotion in favor of less qualified men. She is planning to leave her job to study anthropology.

Lola's profession, filmmaking, is heavily dominated by men. Her successes, swift and exhilarating, have been accompanied by experiences of condescension and humiliation:

> I was on a shoot where the director was a man and his three assistants, the lowest of the low, were women. One of the women was annoying him and he just exploded, "These *fucking* women. I'm just so *fucking* sick of working with you *fucking* women," and he stormed off.

Lola will continue to pay her dues. Her prototypes and her mentors are men, mostly white men. But so what? "I've always had to invent my own life," she says. "If a little girl came to me and said she wanted to be *X*, I'd say to her, 'Know the obstacles, but go for it. Do it, whatever it is.'"

The daughters know that there are still plenty of high school advisers out there, like Jane's, ready to tell girls,

"Oh, you don't need to worry about doing well in math"; like Mary's counselor at her historically black college, who "advised us girls to aim to be secretaries." The daughters know that in spite of so many changes in the world of work, men still earn more than women, and they know that this imbalance threads continuously through history. They have experienced glass ceilings, sexism, tokenism, and "pink ghettos." The fluctuations of the economy also alarm the daughters. Rita Koenig's heart sinks as graduates of her university, one of the country's finest, fruitlessly search for jobs and end up as dishwashers.

But in the daughters' unceasing mental juggling act between optimism and pessimism, optimism wins every time. The optimism they share with Ruth Sidel's young women, however, is not the triumph of media hype over realism. The example of her mother's strength is "enough" for Edith—"Enough for me to believe that I can have the kind of life I told you about. There's no way I can get it if I don't *believe* I can get it. Believing I can get it is a long step toward getting it."

When I ask the daughters whether there is anything they cannot do because they are women, the answer is a resounding, unqualified no. Whether they make conventional or pioneering choices of work, in their book there is no unsuitable job for a woman.

Or, is there? A song from my adolescence throbs in my head like a toothache. Set to a jolly, lilting melody, the words warn that love and marriage, like a horse and carriage, are irrevocably harnessed to one another; reject one, you lose the other as well.

The mothers, like all feminists who preceded them in history, examined the institution of marriage and found it wanting: at worst a prison, a socially sanctioned form of prostitution, a way of infantilizing women and exploiting their labor; at best—a barrier between women and the world, between women and fulfillment, symbol and reality of women's oppression. The mothers pondered—or lived out—the entire gamut of possibilities. Among the mothers who divorced, some remained single by choice, some tried marriage again, some created families of friends, and some found it more satisfying to live with other women. Others undertook the equally arduous task of revising their roles in the marriages they already had. If the daughters have buried Prince Charming as a provider, does he still beckon from the grave as a desirable figure of some sort? Is there a frog out there waiting to be transformed into a suitable mate for the daughter of a feminist?

If only the answers were as easy to sort out as the daughters' attitudes toward work. The subject of marriage is loaded with ambiguity and conflict. Love and marriage, marriage and children are no longer welded together, nor are they completely separated. The combinations shift, vacillate, come together, and separate in complex ways. Even the daughters who are certain they want to marry and have children wrestle with the cautions and reformulations that tormented their feminist mothers.

I ask Jenna, whose fantasy is to spend the next five years on her work "making a difference," to move forward ten or fifteen years into the future.

"Are you wondering if I'm thinking about marriage or kids?" She grimaces. "I know I sound like a cliché, but I really do put my career first. I suppose it's possible to find one person to live with for the rest of my life, but marriage doesn't mean anything to me." This seems surprising, because Jenna and her older sister Rachel regard their parents' relationship as "perfect." Jenna's voice drops to a whisper, as if she were talking to herself: "Gosh, I don't ever want to get married." As for children, she would rather be an aunt to other people's children. "Everyone tells me, oh Jenna, just wait until your biological clock starts ticking away. But I'm going to fight that, because I'd rather put my energy into kids that are already here and that need help."

It does not matter whether their mothers were happily married like Jenna's or unhappily married and divorced several times like Ingrid's; the message that marriage is or could be a "trap"—oppressive and constraining—comes through loud and clear. "I really don't know about men," Ingrid says, shaking her head. "My mom brought me up to believe that marriage is bad, marriage means that your husband owns you. I don't want anyone to own me—ever. Maybe marriage would be nice—if I could find a man who understands that if you love someone you should give them room to grow. It's hard for me to imagine such a man."

"My mother always wished she had been a free spirit, had not married so young, had a career earlier," Adrienne says. "I can't help but think that it stopped her from getting on with her life. I took what my mother said very literally. I was terrified of getting married. I thought my life would end."

Adrienne is thirty-three. She took eight years to decide, but she did marry and finds that her life has not ended. Ingrid is in her early twenties and, of course, she may marry one day. Jennifer will marry "only if I don't feel like I'm compromising my values, my personal goals, to maintain that relationship. I saw my mother's frustrations, a lot of them. In spite of her feminism and her achievements, she had to forego some of her personal goals."

Except for the Jennas, who unequivocally reject marriage—and they are in the minority—the daughters regard marriage as one of several ways to be happy and fulfilled. Over and over I hear, "Well, yes, it would be nice to marry, but it's no big deal if I don't." When I ask Marcia, twenty-nine, about her best fantasy, she answers, "I think I'm a good person, so I hope that in ten years' time I'll continue to be a good person, a good, caring person." Then she talks about work—she can't imagine life without work—and how relationships fit into her life.

"Relationships are very important to me. I have a lot of friends and I hope that in ten years I'll have more friends."

I don't want to feed her lines, but finally, impatient, I ask her about marriage.

"Oh, that's a tough one," she says, laughing. "I'd like to be married. I'd like to experience that. But it's never been the first thing on my mind."

Marcia is a deputy sheriff working the night shift. She needs the daytime hours to finish her bachelor's degree and to care for her foster son and daughter, both three years old. She is in the process of adopting them. Nina articulates what Marcia lives out: "I can see myself as a mother sooner than I can see myself as a wife." Holly feels the same way: "I love kids, and I'd like to have them. First foster children and then my own. I think I'd like to get married, but if I don't, that's OK."

Feminism has loosened the stranglehold of biology as destiny; it does not occur to the daughters who reject motherhood to think of themselves as freaks. But as the daughters scan the horizon, only a few can imagine a life without children. For the lesbian daughters no less than for the heterosexual daughters, children are a major element in their fantasies.

Olivia, twenty-four, came out when she was eighteen. Now she is enrolled in a prestigious culinary school. Her wit, her ready, infectious laugh, have me in stitches throughout the interview, and I'm not surprised when she tells me that she hopes her culinary training will be a ticket to the world. "I'd love to travel around to Third World countries to learn their cuisines. And I want to try being a truck driver and to own property in the mountains," she says. "And, oh, most of all, I want children. I foresee that in about ten years' time. I visualize that very strongly, it's a very passionate thing for me."

The mothers grew up believing that having or raising children alone was a misfortune. For the daughters, it is a plausible option. If they remain unmarried, they are prepared to have children on their own. They rarely see single parenting as the most desirable option, but they prefer it to not having children at all. We have seen how fiercely the daughters guard their right and obligation to take care of themselves. It extends to their potential children as well. After all, as Ingrid says, "Men come and go. Even if I had a great relationship, I'd have to know that I could take care of that child for the rest of my life, because the man may not be around forever."

They do not speak about single motherhood frivolously. They understand that there is more to having a kid than feeding it. Does a child need two parents, they wonder. Probably, but not certainly. The majority of daughters from mother families do not feel incomplete or deprived. "The prospect of having kids alone really scares me," Jennifer confesses. "Still, I'm confident that I could do it. If there were things I couldn't give my child, I'm sure I could find a way to compensate. I can't be all things, but I can sure be a lot of things."

"Sure, I'd have a kid by myself," says Olivia. "But only if I had the finances, *and* I'd need a community, friends. I'd like to have men and women around so the child could get a lot of different influences. Like I had."

Would they agree with Simone de Beauvoir's conclusion that "on the whole marriage today is a surviving relic of dead ways of life"? Dear Simone de Beauvoir: except for the daughters who reject marriage outright (and sometimes, but not necessarily, reject children as well), the idea of marriage is alive and well among the daughters of feminists—or if not exactly well, certainly alive.

For many daughters, marriage is as important in their fantasies as work. Why, then, as they choreograph their futures, don't they say in one breath "I-want-a-career-and-a-family"? They talk about work first in part because they can do it in a way that was unthinkable for their mothers. However the daughters reassemble the elements or reinvent the package, they heave a huge collective sigh of relief that their mothers' generation liberated them from the pressures to marry early and to consider marriage their only vocation. Heather grimaces, reflecting that at her age, twenty-six, her mother was long married, with three children. "Looking back at what I was like when I was twenty, I think it would have been crazy, *crazy,* to be married then—or even now."

The medical technology that prevents unwanted pregnancy and that makes it reasonable to have children in one's thirties and forties never comes up in the daughters' reflections. Rather, they speak about work first because they believe that it is prudent—necessary—to prepare the soil.

"I've always wanted a family as well as a career. But if you'd asked me about my fantasy five years ago, I would've talked about work first because I was just starting out," Linda explains. "I've worked really hard in the last five years to get a name for myself in my field. Now I can start thinking about a family."

Liza, twenty-five, has studied Japanese, acted, and written a novel. Writing is her calling, academia will be her home, and she is about to begin graduate school. "The reason work took precedence is that I didn't know how to work, I had to figure it all out. I have now. I'm confident about work. I'd like to get married as soon as I have a job."

The daughters speak first about work because, ironically, it is easier than talking about marriage. Planning one's career appears to have a logic, a sequence. The rough drafts can be composed and recomposed; you may think you want to be a corporate lawyer and then decide that you want to be a teacher. You anticipate that your path will be strewn with obstacles and you invent tactics to get around them. The process is, or seems to be, under your control. Marriage is a more hazardous, unpredictable business.

The daughters do not regard marriage as the be-all and end-all of life. But if they're going to do it, they're going to do it the old way, at least in form. The form is nuclear and monogamous. The content of marriage, however, has little in common with the "surviving relic" that Simone de Beauvoir was prematurely kissing goodbye.

The daughters whose parents' relationships evolved from the traditional to the innovative, from me-Tarzan-you-Jane into a more equitable collaboration, feel both blessed and burdened by the example: blessed to have had such fathers and burdened by the expectations it leaves them with. Rachel refuses to settle for a husband unwilling "to make the same kind of sacrifices as my father did, and as I'll have to, to attend to a family." She grieves now as she separates from her boyfriend of eight years because "in daily life he was a lot like my father. He was so different from the boyfriends and husbands of my women friends, very unsexist. He cooked and cleaned and gave me a lot of respect." But he could not imagine accepting equal responsibility for children. Finding a man who does "feels pretty impossible" to Rachel.

Antonia Atkins suspects that perfection is like the horizon, always beyond her reach no matter how fast she runs toward it. The lay of the land, however, between where she stands and the horizon begins is very important. "I have to marry someone sort of like my dad. He's a great feminist. But you know, he was raised in a sexist culture like everyone else, so he's always learning too. God, I struggle with so many feminist issues, can I blame a man for the same thing? As long as he'd be willing to work at it."

The daughters who grew up in mother families assume that their parents divorced at least in part because the fathers were not "willing to work at it." If these daughters are going to marry, it will have to be to someone like the other daughters' feminist fathers, or preferably someone even better.

In the daughters' fantasies Prince Charming is their own mirror image: a perfect democrat. He has an emotional commitment to family equal to theirs and he is prepared to translate it into the nitty-gritty of daily life: "fifty-fifty," "equal shares," "taking turns." Holly explains that she does not want a mate like her father, who "helped out" only when her mother was "stressed out." The daughters want a mate who instinctively and consistently shares responsibility for daily life, not just "when I freak out." The ledger need not be balanced every day. Christine thinks about it this way: "We couldn't do fifty-fifty all the time. Sometimes one person has to do forty and the other sixty, depending on what's going on in their lives. Sometimes you have to help the other person out." But in the long run the ledger is balanced: "Whatever job has to be done, we both have to be willing and able to do it."

In 1977 Norman Lear developed a television series called "All That Glitters." It was a spoof on family sitcoms, with a special twist: The husbands stayed home cooking, cleaning, and preening, occasionally whining, and always on the edge of desperation. The wives were the breadwinners, to a woman maniacal about their careers, and alternately condescending toward and exasperated by their husbands' demands for time, affection, attention, and affirmation. The absurdity of gender stereotypes was delicious. Alas, the series ran only three months. I ask the daughters, as long as we are talking about fantasies, how they would feel about a househusband. This, after all, is a test of the democratic relationships they espouse.

"You mean like a Mr. Mom?" Amelia laughs, incredulous—but just for a moment. (The question always makes the daughters laugh.) "Sure I could. You know, like if he was some sort of an artist, or doing something else that he lived for. If he's just taking care of the kids and cleaning the toilets and not developing himself, no! That would feel very uneven to me." Every response is a variation on this theme. So deep is the conviction that "he'd have the same problems as I, giving up a career to stay home and raise a family," that a mirror image of the old gender roles is beyond contemplation. Carolyn Heilbrun said it beautifully: "If men are not boss, women will be. *But this is what men fear, not what women want . . . women do not ask for a new harmony with the major theme always in the soprano range, but for counterpoint*" (my italics).

Beneath this profound commitment to democratic, egalitarian relationships, however, lurks a remnant of older social stereotypes. If not for themselves, then for the "world," it is still somehow unseemly for a man to assume a "feminine" role, and the daughters speak of a stigma on men who take time off from work to be house-husbands. One of Adrienne's female colleagues has just such a marriage: the wife works and the husband is a full-time Mr. Mom. "At work we all make jokes about him, we say we can't believe she married such a lousy bum."

"Would you consider a woman who chose to stay home a lousy bum?"

"No. It's horrible, isn't it, but I'm not immune to a lot of stereotypical thinking."

Who is? More fascinating however, is that as the daughters ponder a future with boyfriends or husbands, they decisively reject simple topsy-turvy, because they do not wish to impose on men what is not desirable or tolerable for women.

Only two daughters spontaneously expressed an interest in something like what feminists of the mothers' generation dreamed, schemed, fantasized about, and sometimes lived—communes, collectives, intentional extended families, utopian communities. Rita Koenig, who is planning to marry a few months after our interview, does not take monogamy for granted, and she is not even sure that it is desirable. "Enduring, definitely," she says about her marriage. "Monogamous, I don't know." People, Rita believes, change throughout their lives, "and those changes could include falling in love with other people. My boyfriend and I agree that you can love two people at once. All we're saying is that we're going to be with each other forever and be friends and supportive and loving."

Rita thinks a lot about alternatives to the nuclear family. "I'm not very impressed with the nuclear family. I question it all the time." She and her boyfriend are already planning to create a communal household "because it would feel so right to share our lives with other families." Nina wants to live, work, and raise her children on a farm "with a bunch of my best friends."

Rita and Nina are discordant voices in the chorus of "monogamous and nuclear." The daughters who want to marry take the nuclear family as much for granted as they do work. They never suggest alternatives; I have to ask. And the answers are dismissive. The nuclear family is no longer oppressive because, they hope, it is egalitarian. That is sufficient for the daughters.

Yet, in spite of the staunch, universal insistence on egalitarianism, by my hoary lights there are a few glitches in the daughters' definitions. Amelia identifies herself without reservations or qualifications as a feminist. My eyebrows shoot up when she proclaims her longing for the traditional family she did not have as the child of a feminist mother. "When I think of the traditional family, I think of the husband, the wife, and the two kids—and I want that. I want that a lot." I push her to describe the inner workings of this traditional family. "Well . . . um . . . I want a partnership, equal shares, equal responsibilities. I'm not going to live my life for my husband or his career, or his success. I need my own. I demand my own." A puzzled grin flits across her face. This is traditional? "I refuse to be superperson. I'll be damned if he's going to come home and put up his feet while I slave over the stove, because I will have been out working hard all day at my job, too."

By this time, Amelia is laughing at herself. Laying it out for me, she hears the dissonance. "Some traditional family!" But to retrieve something of her original formulation, she says that she will take her husband's name. "Somehow taking his name, for me, is a way of bonding." I suggest that they could achieve the same bonding if he took her name. "But then, there goes the traditional. That's a part of the tradition I'd like to keep."

To be sure, a few daughters are adamant about not taking their future husband's name, but for most keeping one's own name is not an indispensable piece of the egalitarian baggage. Linda, already married, reveals that among her friends "it's the first thing you ask when a woman friend is getting married." When Linda took her husband's name, she says her mother was very angry. "Well, not angry, but surprised. I too used to think I would never do it." Linda did it because, like Amelia, "now I feel like I want to create a family, a unity. I don't want different names for my children."

Linda is in the film business and she hyphenates her name for professional purposes, because "I want *my*

name up there." But when her children see her film cred-
its she wants them to see "*their* name up there too."
In other words, her children's name is their father's. Although she willingly, eagerly, assumes her husband's
name in her nonprofessional life, at some level she remains separate, distinct, peripheral to the unity she wants
to create.

Linda never considered asking her husband to take her
name because "there are so many more important things.
The name—it's just a label." The issue has lost the powerful symbolism it had for their mothers. These daughters just toss it off; taking one's husband's name is a trivial
point, not worth bothering about. "It doesn't change
who I am on the inside. I'm still me," says Amanda.

Amelia adds another jarring note to the egalitarianism
she "needs" and "demands." Until her children are two
years old, she will either stop working or work part time.
In unison the daughters *appear* to be demanding of their
fantasy husbands some form of "fifty-fifty" in the allocation of life's chores. They insist that caring for their
babies is no longer a biological imperative. Roaming
through the variations on how children should be cared
for and by whom, the daughters never so much as hint at
feelings of guilt over not being the constant primary parent.

"What bothers me about some feminists is how they
try to create this real Mother Earth imagery," Brenda
fumes. "You know, all maternal, all nurturing." But the
daughters are also telling me in unison that they expect
to stay home with their infants for three months, six
months, a year, two years.

"So you consider the children to be your responsibility?" I ask Amelia.

"It's not that it's my responsibility. I *want* it."

What would she do if her husband wanted to stay home with the little ones?

"Then he should. I'd be home the first year, and he could stay home the second." She sighs. "I'd love that."

When the daughters of feminists say egalitarian, they mean equally parceling out the fun as well as the burdens. To relinquish their children to their husbands feels like a deprivation. Nina reminisces about how she and an old boyfriend discussed a future together. He gingerly suggested that if they married she could work and he could stay home with the baby. "And I said, 'Hey wait a minute, I want to be with the kid too.' I don't want to miss out on that." A year before our interview Susan returned to university. Her husband, a graduate student in finance, offered to stay home for a year with their two small daughters so she could attend school full time. "And he really meant it." Susan glows. "I fell completely in love with him all over again."

Susan describes her friends' reaction to Jason's offer— that is, she emphasizes, her friends who are not feminists.

> I got a lot of doomsday predictions: "Oh, you wouldn't be able to handle that; Oh, he wouldn't be happy; Oh, you mustn't do it." I really think they were threatened by it because their husbands would never make such an offer.

In the end, she did reject his offer, but not because she couldn't "handle it" in quite the way her friends predicted. "I don't want to come home at five, see the kids for a few minutes before they go to bed, and then work until late at night. My dream is for both of us to have time with the children."

But for all their brave fantasies, the daughters share Jennifer's gnawing suspicion that "men have not been taught to value and enjoy children as much as women have." The daughters staunchly believe that they are entitled to egalitarian marriage, but they may still need a little bit of luck to achieve it. The odd man who openly dreams about family as they do still elicits astonishment, gratitude, respect. Such men surely exist—like Nina's boyfriend, Susan's husband—but the daughters believe you have to scratch around to find them.

What about the daughters for whom marriage, and sometimes marriage and children, are no longer fantasy— the daughters who are doing it, or have done it? When Susan married, she expected "fifty-fifty." She and her husband-to-be discussed it endlessly, and he dutifully worked his way through a list of books on feminism and egalitarian relationships.

"Do you have what you expected?" I ask Susan.

"I knew it would be hard. Yeah, it's all a hassle. You know, it's still nicer for him to be taken care of. But we agree on the principles and then we fight it out. See, he has a very clear sense of what's fair, and in the end he always comes through. It's not as egalitarian as I'd like, but we're pretty close."

The daughters and their husbands "hassle" just as their parents did before them. But they begin many rungs higher on the ladder that stretches toward the ideal. They do not negotiate over the principles of egalitarian relationships; the task is putting the principles into practice. I am certainly not surprised to learn that the daughters of feminists have chosen husbands who accept these principles, at least in theory, just as those who are not yet married or coupled plan to do. Rachel, who has just left her boyfriend of eight years, grieves mainly over relinquishing a man who in many important ways is "extremely unsexist." "In daily life he was very different from the boyfriends and husbands of my women friends. He cooked and cleaned as a matter of course." Just as important to Rachel, "He was unaggressive, accepting, and gave me a lot of respect. It was wonderful to be with a man who is not a sexist in that area."

But somewhere, there was an emotional vacuum in their relationship: "He didn't support me in things I need to deal with in myself. It's not part of his world." It also was not part of his world to go with Rachel for counseling. A gender difference? Rachel thinks so. And she hasn't much faith in finding a man whose world meshes better with hers. "I can't imagine having a family with someone—probably modeled after my father—who is unwilling to be there and make the same kind of sacrifices as I to have a family. It feels pretty impossible."

Adrienne, for whom deciding to marry at all was an agony of conflict, begins the day with her husband like this:

> We discuss what needs to be done. Maybe I'll say I have some free time today, I can buy the groceries. What do you think we should get? Or I'll say, today there's just no way, I'm really busy. And he'll do it.

"Who takes responsibility for knowing that the shopping has to be done, and what has to be purchased?" I ask.

"I'd say I do two-thirds of the time. But sometimes he takes full charge of everything."

"And the parenting?"

"I'm lucky. He's really good and really loves our daughter. When we get home from work we share the responsibility." Then Adrienne sighs. "I know this sounds like a cliché, but if our daughter falls down and cries and he's tired or whatever, I'm really the one who has to. . . . That's the bottom line."

Yes, there is a bottom line—a stop sign, a roadblock. Beyond it the negotiations over egalitarianism either do not take place at all or take place without a map. There is a lot of uncharted territory left. Linda is a film editor, her husband is in advertising. They live a frenzied New York City life, without much leisure or social life. Linda, who considers her whole life to have been a course in Women's Studies, reckons that she does more than her husband. "Sometimes, if I'm working really hard, I'll tell him to do the laundry, and he does it. But he wouldn't take it on himself to do it. He doesn't care if the clothes are dirty, so why should he do it? I'm more aware of what needs to be done."

The daughters are uneasy about imposing their standards of cleanliness and order on their mates. They haven't quite figured out whether they are succumbing to traditional stereotypes or whether their greater concern for domestic responsibility is simply a difference in the couple's personalities. "I don't know how to separate them," says Linda. She and her husband eagerly look forward to having children. I'm taken aback when she says that although "he'd love to stay home and take care of the kids while I work," she is the one who will adjust her work life to accommodate a child. She offers two reasons. First, in her profession there are periods when she can legitimately not work without losing the reputation she has so carefully built up. Second, "he talks

like taking care of a kid is easy. I'm not sure he's up
to it."

"Is he physically disabled?"

Linda laughs. But we have touched her bottom line
and she will not cross it.

Like Linda's husband, Amy's live-in boyfriend (they
married shortly after our interview) is very keen on having children. He is even more comfortable with children
than Amy is and would be pleased to take an equal part
in their upbringing, including "the diapers and all that
stuff." But Amy has the same concerns that Linda does:
"I worry that he'll decide to work late and forget to come
home and give the kids dinner if I don't think about it."

Are these gender differences or simply personality differences? Amy is a worrier; her boyfriend is not. Linda
cares about clean clothes; her husband does not. We all
know men who are chronic worriers and women who
don't care about clean clothes. How does one sort out
the personality differences that may have nothing at all to
do with traditional gender expectations? Take note, however—the personality differences always seem to come up
over issues of domestic order, cleanliness, and child care,
and it is still the daughters who are "more aware of what
needs to be done."

For all their passionate commitment to work and career, the daughters who want a family have Plan B in
mind: work that makes room for family obligations and
family pleasures. Someday Amy, the corporate success,
will leave the structured corporate world to be a free-
lance consultant who works at home; Amanda, the industrial designer, will free-lance from her home studio;
Lola will produce films from a studio in her house; and so
on and so on.

The daughters know that there are other serious obstacles to translating egalitarian principles from the head (and heart) into daily life. Stubborn economic realities and the structure of the work world do not yield to feminist notions of family democracy. "Men still make more money than women. And in this country family isn't important," Susan says bitterly. "There should be flexible jobs. Enough money for women *and* men to decide whether to stay home or go to work. I don't think men would choose to stay home now, but they would after a while if it were really an option." To the daughters, creating those options seems a task so daunting, a goal so unattainable, that they can only rely on their individual talents, strengths, and good fortune to make their dreams come true. For them, it is a private struggle.

CHAPTER FOUR

Femininity: Burden or Celebration?

But when you look at yourself in the mirror, I hope you see yourself. Not one of the myths. Not a failed man—a person who can never succeed because success is basically defined as being male—and not a failed goddess, a person desperately trying to hide herself in the dummy Woman, the image of men's desires and fears. I hope you look away from those myths and into your own eyes, and see your own strength.

—URSULA K. LE GUIN, *DANCING AT THE EDGE OF THE WORLD*, 1990

Liza Atkins and I sit at the kitchen table consuming great quantities of icy lemonade. The window blinds filter the sunlight of a hot summer afternoon in upstate New York. Like any sensible person in such weather, Liza is dressed in a tank top, shorts, and sandals. She wears faint lipstick and dangling earrings. She looks healthy, strong, and vibrant. We are talking about feminism's attack on the tyranny of beauty.

The Atkins family, five daughters and a feminist mother and father, spent years around this very kitchen table discussing—and denouncing—the sexist standards of conventional female beauty. "My mom had suffered from those sexist standards. She gave them up. And she didn't want us to be stuck back in high spike heels and that kind of thing." The Atkins daughters rejected those standards before they even acquired them.

But each of the daughters, spontaneously and in her own way, tells me how the first fissure opened in the family consensus. It was the day that Anne, the eldest sister, bought a pair of dangling earrings. "I was twelve," Liza recalls, "and Anne was thirteen. We all considered dangling earrings to be highly sexist, and we gave Anne a really hard time about them." But before long, baubles dangled from the ears of all the Atkins daughters.

In the last year of high school, buffeted between peer pressure and the family's feminist perspective, Liza began to wear "a little mascara"—on the sly. "I'd put it on when I left the house and take it off before I got home. My mom would never have said anything about it, but inside I felt I was failing her."

The world seems not to have noticed Liza's cautious forays into beautification. She enrolled in an Ivy League college where, she discovered, "I still looked so different from everyone else." By her classmates' standards, Liza was overweight. She sported no hairdo, no fashionable clothes, nothing but a little mascara. She slowly began to change her mind and her appearance. "By now I've shifted dramatically on those issues. I wear makeup sometimes, or tighter clothes. Things that are sexy in a woman. I don't want to fight that battle anymore. I no longer want to give up everything. I want to be seen as a woman."

What is this "everything" that Liza, like her mother, "gave up," and that she now wants to reclaim? When I ask another daughter, Amelia, how she feels about the pressures to look, dress, smell a certain way, her answer spells out what many daughters imply: "I'm a feminist in my heart and my mind, but I'm also a woman and I want to be feminine." What does it mean to the daughters of feminists to be womanly and feminine?

When the mothers were growing up, the answer was clear. To be womanly and feminine was to starve the body or, if that didn't work, to squeeze it into elasticized garments, and then to swaddle and to drape it until it conformed as closely as possible to the image *du jour*. To be a real woman was to transform the body into a "figure." I well remember the dubious compliment paid me by a high school chum: "Your body's not bad, Rosie, but you have a lousy figure."

And there was more. To be womanly and feminine was to slather the face with all the paints, powders, lotions that the human mind and the cosmetic industry could contrive; it was to shear the body of all hair, except on the head and the pubis.

When the mothers were growing up they regarded the rituals of altering their faces and bodies—makeup, fashion, shaving legs and armpits—as an initiation into womanhood. This initiation differed from all others that signaled the passage from childhood to adulthood. It was not, for example, like the bar mitzvah—get to the right age, say the right prayers, and presto! you are a man. Women's rites of passage required that the ceremonies be performed every single day (at least once) throughout life, because at heart women believed what H. L. Mencken once said so well and so nastily: "The average woman, until art comes to her aid, is ungraceful, misshapen, badly calved and crudely articulated, even for a woman. If she has a good torso, she is almost sure to have bad teeth. If she has good teeth, she is almost sure to have scrawny hands, or muddy eyes, or hair like oakum, or no chin." For the mothers, the rites of feminine passage were never-ending; you never arrived. One year fashion dictated that makeup be flamboyant and obvious, another year that it be discreet and "natural." But going without makeup was not an option.

The feminist movement rebelled against the tyranny of beauty as vigorously as it staked a claim to a life outside the kitchen. Indeed, the rebellion and the claim were bound up in each other. If a woman has as much right as a man to work outside the home, it is because she is more than a "sex object," as we used to say. A woman's sole purpose in life is not to catch a man with her greatest (always elusive) attribute—beauty—that is itself defined by men.

The goal of the rebellion was not simply to replace girdles with sweat pants, nor was it a denial of aesthetics. Remember, the sixties and seventies witnessed a great aesthetic explosion: beads, spangles, embroidery, feathers, hair, hair everywhere—for men as well as for women. Instead, the goal was to transform the burden of phony femininity into a celebration of innate womanliness. Exactly what that innate womanliness is remained to be discovered. But the search was on.

In the larger culture, the rebellion was a flop. Cosmetic firms aren't moaning about falling sales. The fat farms and exercise salons multiply and thrive. Plastic surgeons proudly correct nature's mistakes, even if, on the way to the bank, they glance nervously over their shoulders at breast implants. Fashion still jerks women about like a yo-yo on a string—up, down, tight, loose.

True, today's rules are less stringent. In the early seventies I taught history at a women's college. At the beginning of one semester a group of women faculty members discussed, almost in whispers, whether we could wear pants to class. We delegated the most respectable woman in the group to cautiously sound out the dean of faculty. The dean responded, well, yes, we perhaps could wear pants as long as we were neat and clean. What a victory! Today daughters rejoice with Nina, who is "so glad that flat-heeled shoes are acceptable now." But almost two decades before the modern women's movement surfaced, Simone de Beauvoir had already gotten it just right: "Precisely because the concept of femininity is artificially shaped by custom and fashion, it is imposed upon each woman from without . . . trousers have become feminine. That changes nothing fundamental in the matter: the individual is still not free to do as she pleases in shaping the concept of femininity."

Feminist mothers did not change the matter in a fundamental way. But they did teach their daughters to question the culture's conviction that beauty is a woman's most significant attribute, and that there is only one way to be beautiful, mainly by means of artifice. For the daughters of feminists, struggling to peel away layers of hype, no conventional method of altering the female form is neutral or taken for granted.

Antonia thinks about her appearance as a woman every day of her life. She must, for she aspires to an acting career. "Sure, I want to look nice. Everyone does. But do you have to wear makeup to look nice?" Antonia tries to sort out the difference between real and artificial. "I struggle with the issue of makeup because I know that if I were on a desert island, I wouldn't wear it."

Ellie muses, "There's nothing wrong with wanting to be attractive to someone you find attractive. But what would it be like to live in a world where women didn't worry about being beautiful to attract men?"

Rita asks bitterly, "What's beautiful? The standards are insane, unrealistic. They make us all feel ugly. My skinny friend doesn't think she's beautiful because she has a little fat around her knees. My dark-haired friend doesn't think she's beautiful because she's not blond, or because her nose is a little funny." Her voice rises. "There is no beautiful. Nobody is beautiful. That's what needs to be reworked—what does beautiful mean?"

Perhaps the purest example of how distasteful the culture finds the unaltered female body is shaving legs and underarms. It comes up spontaneously in every daughter's beauty saga. Antonia's vacillations are typical. Her mother taught her that "it is sexist and unnatural to shave." Heeding her mother, Antonia, pure and hairy, braved the world's disapproval. "It was horrible, horrible. I'd be in shorts, and people would check out everyone's legs, and I'd just die." On the track team in high school and on the crew team in college, her fellow team members displayed smooth armpits in tank tops. Antonia hid her shaggy armpits in shirts with sleeves, but found it extremely uncomfortable to run or row in sleeves.

"I struggled and struggled and finally thought—this is ridiculous. It's just some hair. Big deal." Antonia shaved, "still hoping someday to be strong enough not to care." Then, she recounts, came the big breakthrough. She began to go swimming without shaving. "And by now, in fact, I don't shave my legs or my pits. Never! When people notice, I say, 'Never Been Shaved.' " She grins, raising her arm in a gesture of triumph.

Antonia's younger sister Mia shaved her legs and armpits in high school. "My mom was against it, but I couldn't help thinking that hairless legs and underarms are beautiful. I was totally confused. I even considered shaving one leg and not the other. *That* would really throw people off." Now a junior in college, Mia has decided that to shave to please other people violates her principles. "If my body hair turns people off, well, that's their problem."

For some daughters, it's other people's problem. But for most it is still "my" problem. "It's so stupid," Linda says. "If we weren't supposed to have hair, we wouldn't have it." Linda spent some years in Los Angeles hanging out on the beach. "It got so that I just didn't want people to see my hairy legs. And then, little by little, shaving just began to make me feel good." Even as she yields to "what is acceptable," she debates with her husband. "I say to him, you don't have to shave your legs, why do I? But if I don't do it, I don't feel right. It's been bored into my head."

Other daughters follow Linda's path, but explain their choice differently. In high school and college Jennifer and her friends "endlessly" discussed whether shaving meant "making yourself into a sex object." Now, several years out of college, Jennifer says that "if I feel like shaving my legs once in a while—not very often—I'm not going to kick myself over it." As an African American, she is experienced in solving puzzles over appearance. "Being black, I have had to go through all sorts of issues of appearance, like hair straightening." Now she believes that she has transformed racist and sexist imperatives into choices, burdens into celebrations. "We live in an age of choice. If you know your history, as a woman and as a black, you have many ways to be strong. The freedom to choose how you want to look is a strength. I don't think the point of the women's movement was to force me to struggle over whether to shave my legs, but to give me the freedom to choose." She thinks of her appearance as "a form of personal expression" and as a way to "have a little fun."

In every culture people decorate themselves, some of the daughters point out, so it must be part of the natural order of things that daughters like Antonia try so hard to distinguish from the artifice of fashion.

"We all decorate ourselves," Maria says. "Where do you draw the line? Do you bathe? Do you comb your hair? When I decorate myself, it's pleasing to my eye and I know it's pleasing to others."

Ellie's costume of choice is "unisex." On principle she has never worn makeup or shaved her legs, and she didn't wear dresses until she was fifteen. "I don't know what triggered it," she says, "but suddenly, in my junior year at college, I became interested in clothes. Wacky, interesting outfits. I love bright colors, certain materials and textures, and I love to have them around me."

Many daughters tell me that this is one of the choices their mothers struggled to provide for women. "I'd hate it if everyone wore the same thing," Rita says. "Choice! Choice! Everyone, men and women, should have the same options. That's my goal: we should all have the same options for colors, styles, masculine, feminine, long, short, dresses, pants." Liza, like Rita, pities men for having so few choices: "I love it when men wear fancier clothes or jewelry. It's too bad that their options are so limited."

This sounds like androgyny, but when I introduce the word most of the daughters slide past it. It is all but absent from their vocabulary. One daughter, however, uses the word as "high praise." Hilary is a lesbian. She wrestles with the conflict between her ideal of androgyny and the constraints of sexist convention. Can she dress her year-old son in ruffles and flowered clothing? "I'd like him to wear all sorts of things, but I have a distinct fear of somebody saying, 'Oh, you're trying to make him a girl.'" She wrestles with it for herself as well. "I think decorating yourself is natural and fun. But when only one gender is expected to decorate itself for the pleasure of the other, and when you're crippling yourself to do it, that's a horror."

Saluting womanhood with clothes, makeup and "choice! choice!" is like going to a party and wondering if you will have to pay a cover charge. Two daughters have been raped; several have been mugged and threatened with rape; all have been "hassled." Shanna's eyes blaze: "I *hate* walking down the street and being hassled by men. I *hate* dealing with that shit every single day. Men think you don't feel it every day." When I interview Maureen she is wearing a miniskirt. "I wouldn't walk out on the street dressed like this," she says. "I have to dress a certain way, have a certain posture, act a certain way, so that men won't think I'm looking for something. I resent that. A lot." Some daughters devise a camouflage to minimize their fear of vulnerability. Ellie, the lover of bright colors and interesting textures, confesses, "I feel more vulnerable if I'm wearing a skirt or even nail polish. I never wear high heels. It's too dangerous." A few years ago Linda cut her hair very short and wore leather jackets; "It was my shell. I felt I had to look really tough just to get to and from work."

Linda and Ellie live in New York City, Maureen and Shanna live in other large, dense urban areas. Even in a bucolic part of California, Nina feels that she has to protect herself from "the hounds, the land sharks." Several years ago Nina was raped. She knows that you don't have to look or "come on" a certain way to be raped. She knows, as all women know, that old women are raped; women who don't wear makeup are raped; women in dowdy clothes are raped. The daughters know one thing and believe another.

The daughters still believe, all evidence to the contrary, that if they are hassled, mugged, or raped, they must answer for it. Before the rape, Nina reminisces, "I used to dress very differently—tank tops and miniskirts. Now I realize that regardless of what you think or of who you are, what you wear puts out a message. And you need to take responsibility for that." Only when Nina is in a rebellious mood does she say to herself, "Fuck it! I'm going to dress however I want. I want to yell out—you have no right to hassle me. Just leave me alone!"

So much for choice.

Dressing up and making up may be fun, a celebration, a means of self-expression, and some daughters may choose to pay the price, real or imagined. Weight is an entirely different issue. Except for the few daughters blessed with a benevolent metabolism, weight is still a source of unrelenting anxiety, hovering over the daughters like a bird of prey, threatening to swoop down and peck away at their "image," to spoil their lives or at the very least their mood. "Weight is a big issue. I don't think about it every day—only every other day." Judith sighs.

Maria began to worry about her weight as an adolescent and she still worries "all the time." I ask her to look at photographs of herself when she was younger. "When you look at them now, was there ever a need to worry?" She shakes her head. "No, never. Oh, this is so hard. I still think of myself as ten pounds overweight."

For many of the daughters, losing weight and being slim have layers of meaning that have nothing to do with aesthetics. Jane spins a harrowing narrative of obsession and deprivation that began when she gained weight after the birth of her second child. "I figured that before I could go back to school, before I go out in public, I had to do something for my image."

"Well," I offer cautiously, "you have another alternative. You could just say, hey, I'm chubby [she isn't] and I'll go out and get new clothes and live with it and—"

"No," she interrupts firmly. "That is *not* acceptable to me. Losing weight is a real test for me. It helps me to believe that if other hard things come along, I'll have the strength to struggle through them."

Liza's weight has plagued her since she was fifteen, and for two years in late adolescence she was bulimic. Now, although according to the charts she carries some excess weight, "the more I like myself, the less important it becomes." Less important, but hardly unimportant. Liza believes that liking herself, and therefore caring less about her weight, means that she has relinquished the need to be "perfect." Liza has not redefined perfect; it still means thin.

And, Liza earnestly adds, "I'd only gain a lot of weight

again if I were full of self-hatred. When I don't like myself I do bad things to my body." "Bad things" means gaining weight. Gaining weight means self-hatred. It is a vicious circle. To the degree that the perfect slim body eludes them, daughters like Jane and Liza are convinced that they lack character. "If you can't control your weight, what can you control?" Rita asks. Control of one's body becomes visible, public testimony to one's virtue.

Side by side with the tribulations of weight, the daughters enjoy the pleasures of strength and health. It is hard to remember, unless you are a feminist mother, that not so very long ago physical prowess (especially if it *showed*) was the last thing on a woman's mind. Two daughters, describing their adolescence, tell me that they were "tomboys." For most of the daughters, however, the word *tomboy* is archaic. It no longer describes a special, aberrant kind of female. Antonia runs track and rows crew, Hilary bicycles and plays softball, Liza does gymnastics, and many of the daughters try to fit some form of exercise into their schedules.

When we talk about weight Lola says that "I have it in perspective. I'd rather look healthy than gorgeous." Jennifer, who has struggled with both sexist and racist norms of beauty, and who concludes that appearance is a form of self-expression, wants above all to look "comfortable, strong, and capable." Recall Amelia, "a feminist in my heart and my mind" who "also wants to be feminine." Amelia wants to look "pretty—and strong." But Liza is embarrassed to confess that she exercises to a Jane Fonda tape, because she understands the subtext to the story of strength and health. You can be as strong as Jane Fonda, but if you don't look like her, strength is irrelevant.

I pore over the transcripts of the daughters' recorded interviews many times before I realize how often they use the word *image*. Webster tells us that an image is an *imitation* of a person or a thing—a representation, a visual impression, a concept. It suggests the real thing, but it never is the real thing. It is like a shadow—it can be projected or altered, if you stand a certain way at a certain time of day. But substance and shadow are destined forever to be separate. Some daughters understand this well. "I know how insane this image business is," says Rita, who has devised a little game to test her own perceptions. "I'll look in the mirror and think I look OK. I'll go downstairs and eat a piece of chocolate cake. Then I'll go back to the mirror. I look fat."

Honoring her mother's feminism, Liza Atkins "gave up everything" as an adolescent—makeup, fashion, diets—but as a young woman she feels liberated by accepting more conventional standards of beauty. Most daughters take the other way around. Adrienne at age thirty-three talks about how her weight plagued her in her twenties. "What surprised me in my twenties when I thought about feminist issues was how little things had changed, how much women still hated their bodies. Me too. My body and I were enemies. Now we're friends. So now I can say, 'Oh, my butt looks too big today. So what!' My looks occupy a smaller and smaller place as I get older."

Maureen remembers that as she was growing up, her mother was on a perpetual diet. "Maybe that's where I got that obsession," she speculates, adding that together she and her mother have gone through a process of re-evaluation. "Now my mom just can't stand to hear me or my sisters say that we're fat, or that we feel fat. She says we should understand that we're perfect the way we are." Maureen, like her mother, has made friends with her body. "The other day I told my mom that I'm much more comfortable with my appearance than I was a couple of years ago. I could have a lot of other things to worry about. I could be missing my right hand, or have cancer, or a lot of other problems worse than being three or four pounds overweight." With a shrug of irritation, she bursts out, "Oh, I wish the pressure of being thin and lanky and beautiful would just die off. I wish *Glamour* and *Vogue* would just go out of business."

"Funny you should ask me about weight," Nina says. The night before our interview she and three friends had been up all night discussing how much their image is determined by what others think. "For me it boils down to the way my mother brought me up. Yes, you can influence me by your standards, but ultimately I have an inner core of strength. You can't ruin me because you think my hips are too big."

The most recent edition of Webster's dictionary defers to a late-twentieth-century reality. One definition of image—the concept, the representation—is something "often deliberately created or modified by publicity, advertising, etc." When I encourage the daughters to think about who or what creates the images that so influence them, they point a finger (or raise one) at the media. The daughters are disgusted with the media's pernicious aims and manipulative methods. "It's just a multimillion dollar industry that makes money by making women feel insecure," Mia fumes.

On her bulletin board Cary Atkins keeps two ads clipped from a popular fashion magazine. One ad displays a chastely stylish woman in a form-fitting green dress—"You know, incredibly skinny, the way women are supposed to look." The other ad shows a voluptuous woman seemingly writhing out of her bikini and off the page. "This is enough to drive you crazy," Cary grumbles, pointing to the bathing beauty. "There's no way this woman could fit into that green dress. It wouldn't even fit over her thighs."

For the daughters, media has become another word for the entire culture. The media, the culture, speak with a forked tongue. Feminist mothers sometimes did as well. Now Maureen's mother scoffs at the great goddess of slimness, but she was always on a diet while Maureen was growing up. Marcia's mother wears high heels to work and "still thinks that casual dressing means not buttoning the top button of her blouse." In Adrienne's eyes, her mother is beautiful, but her mother is still uneasy about her own appearance and about Adrienne's as well. "She'll say to me, 'Why don't you shave your legs, honey. We're having a party.' I call her on it, and she says, 'It's not about feminism, it's about looking good.' "

Mothers who begged their daughters not to shave their legs "because it'll just grow in thicker, and then it'll *really* be an issue," were encouraging their daughters to challenge fashion's despotism; but they were also acknowledging that, as one staunchly feminist mother admonished, "gorilla legs" are unseemly for a woman. With one foot in the culture and another in the process of bucking the culture, mothers could only transmit the struggle, not the solution.

So, I suggest to the daughters, let's get closer to home. Granted, the entire culture, and its modern spokes-thing, the media, creates images of beauty and persuades, cajoles, threatens women into refashioning themselves to conform to those images. But whom are you really trying to please?

Only themselves, a few daughters insist. "A lot has to do with society and image, but some of it is just personal," Rita says. She speculates about aesthetics and concludes that everyone has some innate aesthetic sensibility, as if it were encoded in our genes. But for most daughters personal aesthetics cannot be isolated from social norms. Recall Antonia's insight that she would not wear makeup on a desert island. "I use that example a lot when I argue with women friends. And they say, 'Oh no, I'd wear makeup on a desert island, because I do it for myself, to feel good.' Give me a break," Antonia scoffs. "You're not doing this for yourself at all."

For whom, then?

"I've always thought that women dress more to please other women than to please men," Maria says. She puts it in a positive light: "We want to look nice for each other." I ask her whether her women friends would no longer love her if she stopped shaving her legs, stopped wearing makeup, and dressed only in sweat suits. After a pause, she says, "Well, no, of course they wouldn't. But they'd say something's wrong. They'd say I'm not caring about myself. Something's not functioning right." Looking "right" is a sign of mental health.

Maureen describes her relationship with a woman friend. "She's really thin. She's neurotic about it, but she always looks great, always perfectly dressed too. Sometimes I don't care how I look, and I go to school dressed any old way. I don't even think about it until I run into her. And then I worry about what she'll think."

"It's women who say it's disgusting if you don't shave your legs. Or that you should lose weight, you should do this, you should do that," Liza complains. Why is this so? The question always elicits a long, reflective pause. The inevitable answer is that women, in complicated ways, are often only doing men's dirty work. Men set the standards and women enforce them.

Mia believes that women put other women down to elevate their own sense of attractiveness. "Women look at other women and tear them apart: 'Eww, why is she wearing that? She looks like such a slob.' They do it to convince themselves that they're more attractive to men. That's only on the surface. Underneath, it's true, I don't dress for women. I dress to attract men."

Renata could wear the proverbial sack cloth and still turn heads. She calls herself a sucker: "I buy into a lot of that 'looksist' bullshit. I know that I shouldn't be getting my confidence from it, but at a lower level it makes me feel good. Yeah, it's really oppressive. Women's fashion and women's beauty are really men's idea of fashion and beauty."

Anne-Marie cuts close to the bone. In the kind of limbo that often precedes a marital break, Anne-Marie's husband was having a blatant flirtation with a fellow worker. "I showed up at his office one day and saw her. She was so cute and blond, in a little short skirt and makeup just so. I thought, well, I'm just garbage; I didn't try hard enough, I didn't exercise enough to look like her, I didn't wear enough makeup. Then I got really angry at him. I'm perfectly fine, I thought. If that's what he wants, then I don't want him."

Once in a while the abstract man who orchestrates the cacophony of images, demands, standards turns out to be something different in the flesh. Judith recalls that she gained fifty pounds while backpacking for a year in Europe. "I had a wonderful, passionate relationship with a guy that year. My sister asked me whether I minded being fat, and I said no. Here's this person that I love and it doesn't make any difference to him." Nicole fell in love with a man who "loved me just the way I was, and best when I didn't wear any makeup. So I stopped." But the occasional experience of being loved regardless of one's weight and appearance is no match for the power of the culture. Today Judith thinks about weight every other day. Nicole provides an epilogue to the love affair that liberated her: as the relationship soured "I started looking to physical beauty again and comparing myself to other women."

When I interviewed Rachel she was leaving her live-in boyfriend of eight years. "The security of the relationship protected me from all the negative expectations of women's image in the world." Now Rachel is on the market and "suddenly I have to prove that I'm worthy." For the first time in her life she shaves her legs, perms her hair, and worries about her weight. "I feel sick about it. I ask myself, why am I doing this? To feel good about myself? It's a delusion, I know. And it's confusing and disabling. But at this point in my life, it feels better just to let go of it."

The man in the flesh is here today, gone tomorrow; the imaginary man who wants his woman to conform to some combination of painted, skinny, "sexy," and fashionable is everywhere. Amanda's boyfriend of the moment may prefer her unadorned, but at a staff meeting one of her fellow workers publicly announced that "If I ran this office, I'd make every woman wear Spanish 'fuck-me' pumps." Amanda does not have a personal relationship with this colleague. She doesn't even like him. But he speaks for the imaginary man, and his compelling voice is deeply internalized. He is everywhere because he is within every woman's mind.

What about the daughters who really do strive to attract and please only other women? Debby, now twenty-nine, has gone through many "incarnations" in her appearance. She experimented with makeup, "dabbled" with shaving her legs, and violently seesawed over her weight. In the nine years since she came out as a lesbian to herself and the world—"in stages"—she has made peace with her body. "No more diets ever again," she says. Since she is concerned only with pleasing her partner—a woman—Debby feels free to decorate herself in ways "that I wouldn't be caught dead doing with a man."

Have the lesbian daughters, then, evicted the imaginary man as well as the corporal man? Of course not, says Hilary, who was bulimic at the age of sixteen—precisely when she had her first relationship with a woman. Now twenty-eight and long past the obsession with her weight, she still has what she calls a "weight consciousness." And, she adds, "I don't know any woman who doesn't." The imaginary man—or the media or the culture, whatever one calls the arbiter of women's appearance—still lurks at the periphery of the lesbian daughters' consciousness. But the daughters believe that the lesbian world at least offers options, a variety of refuges from the ubiquitous influence of conventional beauty.

Wherever they draw the line between capitulation and rebellion, not one of the daughters buys the entire conventional beauty package. Linda shaves her legs, but "I just never think about diets or makeup or clothes. I never felt that had anything to do with me." Amelia wears eye shadow, but "you wouldn't catch me dead in a miniskirt or a tight bodysuit." Lola "shlumps around in glasses," but puts her contact lenses in and wears lipstick for special occasions. Becky, now twenty-two, always shaves her legs. But she stopped wearing makeup when she was sixteen, and she feels just as "confident" in hiking boots and jeans as in a dress.

The mothers, taught to sacrifice comfort for beauty's sake, unlearned the lesson as they studied feminism. The daughters have incorporated comfort into their own definition of femininity. In a curious way it influences their choices in that critical area of their lives, work.

Nina turned away from an acting career because it involved "too much ego, appearance, image." Now an environmental educator, she comfortably roams the California seashore in shorts and hiking boots. Once in a while she wears makeup; "a little purple around my eyes, a little fluorescence on my lips," because "it's fun to dress up once in a while."

"What would you do," I ask, "if you had a job that required that you wear elegant clothes, high heels, and makeup?"

Nina squints, trying to imagine herself in such an outlandish getup. "I would never wear high heels," she says firmly. "That's too uncomfortable. On the other hand, if I were working for an incredible environmental organization and I had to travel around and lobby, and I really felt that I was affecting people's lives . . . so, OK, maybe I'd have to wear clothes that are less comfortable. I'd have to balance what I was giving up with what I was getting in return."

Rita, like many other daughters, does not believe that any job is worth the compromise. "If an employer said I had to wear a dress every day or high heels or makeup,

I'd say forget it! More than forget it. I'd file a suit! It's a very important place to draw the line." Renata calls high heels a form of bondage. "I just wouldn't take a job that required that. I couldn't work productively."

The daughters finesse the problem by choosing work that does not impose an offensive dress code. "You'll notice," Nina points out, "that I haven't chosen to work in a bank." Amanda, an industrial designer, wears trousers and T-shirts—and lipstick—to work. Comfort is on her mind, and so is principle. Her office manager, she tells me, "wears these tight, short Lycra skirts and high heels. It's a manipulative tactic. She wants a three-thousand-dollar raise instead of a two-thousand-dollar raise. She wants something and to get it that's what she does. It's gross. It's disgusting. I'd never do that."

Many of the daughters feel that they are bedeviled by two contenders for mastery over their behavior. One demon whispers in the right ear that to reject conventional "femininity" is to deny their womanliness. The other demon whispers in the left ear that the smallest concession to conventional "femininity" is a surrender to sexism. Lola has chosen to spend her life making documentary films about strong, achieving women. She believes that a dogmatic feminist rejection of conventional "femininity" is no improvement over the tyranny of "horrible media stereotypes" of women. Both party lines judge women by their exteriors, by how they look rather than by what they believe and how they behave. As an African American woman, Lola is painfully aware of what's wrong with that.

Appearance, the daughters are saying, should not be the criterion of one's virtue or of one's commitment to feminist principles. "It's a mistake to divide women that way," Susan says. "It's a way women allow themselves to get divided. If a woman shaves her legs and calls herself a feminist, then she's a feminist."

Liza Atkins is much angrier than Susan. Once, in a college feminist group, she was severely criticized for wearing lipstick. "They told me I wasn't a feminist. Hey! I've been fighting feminist battles since I was born. These women, they found feminism in college, and suddenly they feel they have the right to preach the only way to be a feminist! If you want to be involved in feminism, I say—terrific. And if you want to be a feminist and wear makeup, I say—great."

Rita, among the staunchest torchbearers of the mothers' feminist ideals, feels that the time has passed for judging a woman by her appearance. "That's what men do," she points out. "It's no different from saying a woman is asking to be raped because she dresses a certain way. A woman can wear tight miniskirts, bleach her hair, shave her whole body if she wants to—and still be a good feminist."

The notorious image of bra-burning is an exquisite example of how media voodoo twisted a feminist statement into its opposite. It is probably the single most powerful distortion of the dreams of the mothers' generation. Never mind that such an incident never occurred.* It could have (and I, for one, wish it had). If an actual bra-burning had taken place, this is what it would have meant: Don't tell me that the only way I can be beautiful is if I mash my body into something nature

---

* See Gabrielle Burton, *I'm Running Away from Home But I'm Not Allowed to Cross the Street* (Pittsburgh: Know, Inc. 1972), p. 14. Susan Faludi, *Backlash* (New York: Crown Publishers, Inc., 1991), p. 75.

never intended it to be. Don't tell me that to be a "real" woman I must bind my body as in the past I bound my mind, my spirit, and my life choices to satisfy male fantasies.

One can only marvel at how a fictitious incident that would have honored the unbound, unadorned female form was transformed into a metaphor for the repudiation of "femininity" and for a rejection of aesthetics. But the metaphor is enshrined in the public imagination, and the daughters are as susceptible to it as anyone else. The daughters are a long way from shaping a concept of femininity that is free of sexism, but they firmly believe that they are closer than their mothers were at their age. "It's slow going," Liza says, shaking her head. "I can't say that I reject everything sexist. But I'm much further than my mom was when she was growing up, and my daughters will be even further."

The quest for innate womanliness is like a labyrinth that turns in on itself: we often find ourselves in tunnels that we've already traversed. Perhaps there is no innate femininity. Antonia's desert island is a place in the mind. It yields no clues to what we would value if we lived isolated from human society. In every culture appearance is language; "What you wear puts out a message," as Nina puts it. The questions are who devises the language that culture ascribes to appearance, need it be sexist, and how can we change it?

CHAPTER FIVE

Friendship
and Sex

*Transformative feminism's promise was a world
in which men and women could balance love,
friendship, work, and community; a world that
would encourage cooperation between men and
women and a sense of social responsibility in
citizens, who would recognize their inter-
connectedness and who would affirm rather
than deny their need for relationship.*

—SUZANNE GORDON, *PRISONERS
OF MEN'S DREAMS,* 1991

The women's movement of
the sixties and seventies, the feminist mothers' movement, was not a cult. There were no tests for eligibility,
no secret handshakes or passwords. Nor did a single man-
ifesto encompass every feminist's vision. Out of her own
most deeply felt needs, the feminist of this era pursued
goals that seemed most urgent to her, those things that
she could no longer do without. For some the goal was
economic independence, for others, sexual liberation; the
list goes on. Sometimes the debate over divergent inter-

ests exposed serious disagreements within the movement. To distinguish their particular slant, many women attached adjectives to the word *feminist*: radical, lesbian, socialist—here, too, the list goes on. But all feminists dreamed a common dream, whether or not they expressed it in words or even understood it fully, because the dream followed from each individual pursuit. In the words of Adrienne Rich, "Some of us, calling ourselves radical feminists, never meant anything less by women's liberation than the creation of a society without domination; we never meant less than the making new of all relationships."

In this chapter, we stop at two signposts on the road to that heady vision of social transformation: friendship and sex. What do the daughters of feminists imagine that women and men, and women and women, can be to each other?

Early in my own feminist odyssey I had a moment of startling revelation. Twelve years after my mother's death, I was visiting with Tamara, my mother's best lifelong friend and my beloved friend as well. Then in her middle seventies, Tamara was the last living link to my mother and to my childhood. I exploited her mercilessly: Remember! Remember! Tell! Tell! A flamboyant polyglot, effortlessly slipping in and out of Russian, English, and Yiddish, Tamara careened through episodes and decades, painting in words a splendid picture of female bonding. Every important relationship in her life—and in my mother's life as well—had been with women.

My mother and her pals—immigrant women from another culture—had sisterhood. The American experience was different. In the America of my prefeminist days, other women were the competition. Friendship with women did not confer status. It was not proof of one's worth. Of course, women had women friends, and women probably spent more time with each other than with men because of the sharp delineation between male spheres of work and female spheres of home. But friendship with women was second best. It was even expendable, if it intruded on the relationship with a man that women believed they needed to be a real woman.

The feminists of my generation invented the phrase "Sisterhood is powerful!"; we thought we had invented sisterhood as well. At the time of my visit with Tamara, the deluge of literature exploring women's friendship back almost into prehistoric times had yet to come. It turns out that we had only rediscovered sisterhood, re-created it. In her book *Composing a Life,* Mary Catherine Bateson reminisces about women's consciousness-raising groups of the late sixties and early seventies. She observes that "the greatest discovery of these groups was that other women could be companions rather than rivals. They learned the value of shared experiences and the benefits of solidarity, becoming friends." We exulted in what my mothers' friends had taken for granted. And as we reconnoitered this luxuriant terrain, the landscape of friendship with men began to look pretty arid. Absorbing the rewards of intimacy with women, we wanted to remake our relationships with men in the image of our relationships with women. It didn't quite work. My feminist friends and I are still talking about the complexities and limitations of friendship with men, when we aren't wondering whether it is possible at all.

Except for a couple of daughters who consider themselves loners, who need more solitude than companionship, the daughters place friendship high among life's necessities—and pleasures. The daughters with "enough" good friends feel blessed. The daughters who lack friends feel deprived. Friendships with whom, I ask? At the very first interview, I sit up with a jolt.

Brenda, twenty-one, has just graduated from a women's college on the East Coast. Her intimate circle of friends includes three men and two women. "I feel very close to all of them. I can talk to all of them about anything."

Taken aback, I ask, "So when you think about soul mates, gender is not an issue?"

"No. I think men and women can have the same sensibilities. Sure, in the aggregate women are more able to discuss their emotions than men—that's part of the socialization. But it's not universally true. A lot of women can't, and a lot of men can."

Olivia, a twenty-four-year-old lesbian daughter, has vivid memories of the feminist retreats to which her mother often took her. "They were pretty wonderful events; a lot of strong women, some straight, some gay. I really bonded with them." She remembers "how they used to say you can't trust men. It still reverberates in my head." As she was coming out, Olivia's lesbian community, too, "told me I had to make a choice, men or women. They were all telling me I had to be separatist. I decided, no, that's not real. People are people." Olivia's deepest emotional and sexual bonds are with other lesbians, but she rejects separatism and she has good male friends. The daughters of feminists sound like old-fashioned integrationists.

When Mia's best woman friend meets a man, she immediately asks herself whether he is "boyfriend material," and if he isn't, she loses interest in him. "I don't think like that," Mia says. "After all, most of the men you meet are not going to be boyfriends. So why not try friendship?" She has tried it and she likes it. Mia *expects* men to be her friends.

The evidence accumulates. As much as I doubt the capacity of numbers to reveal meaning, I cannot resist presenting a statistic: of the fifty daughters, only four do not have male friends. None of the heterosexual daughters regard men only as "boyfriend material," and if they don't have male friends, they wish they did. The homosexual daughters also have male friends, straight and gay.

What is an intimate male friend? It turns out that they don't grow on trees, because the daughters and the men they would like to befriend do not always have in mind the same scenario. "It's hard for me to be friends with men, because I always feel like they're checking me out, even before they just talk to me," Jane complains. "I've had male friends," Linda explains, "but all of a sudden they announce that they want something else. So maybe the whole friendship was one thing to them and another to me."

Jenna wants to believe that friendship between women and men can be as strong and intimate as friendship between women, but she can't always convince her potential male friends "to get beyond that sexual tension." "I make it clear from the beginning that I'm not going to sleep with them. I say, listen, we *can* be friends. They try, but something sexual always comes up." Ingrid is almost ready to give up: "Every close friendship I've had with a man has been ruined because he wants to turn it into a sexual thing. I *hate* that."

All the daughters, including those who have deep relationships with *some* men, have had the same disappointing experiences with *many* men. Not surprisingly, the intimate male friends of many of the daughters are gay.

Friendship with men languishes for some daughters when they marry or live with a man. "It's not exactly that my husband would be upset if I had a close male friend," says Linda. "But such a friendship couldn't easily fit into our lives." Ingrid, who has been living with her boyfriend for four years, is more explicit. "It's really hard to have a close male friend now because my boyfriend is so threatened by that." That, too, is a variety of sexual tension.

The daughters who make no distinctions between their men and women friends believe that both the men and the friendships are unusual. Becky describes her friendship with Mark. "I tell him everything. We have the same views and the same hopes. But Mark is special."

In what way, I ask.

"His attitudes about men and women are very liberal. It's not the norm to have a *real* male friend. Neither for me nor for my women friends."

Rachel calls friendship the "substance of my life," and says that she is as close to her male friends as to her women friends. "But it's amazing, really. I'm very different from most of my women friends in that way."

I ask Debby whether she has the same kind of intimacy with her male friends as with her female friends.

"No. Has any woman ever said she did?"

"What is the quality of the difference?"

Debby mentally runs through her address book and chooses her most valued male friend to describe. "I'm very close to Joshua. We talk absolutely openly, we cry and laugh together, we talk all night, we play and dance. But eventually, men reveal some level of insensitivity.

There's some deep inner core that's missing. Some know-ingness."

The precise nature of that "knowingness" eludes the daughters. It's like trying to translate music or painting into speech. "I just feel like there's something about inner experiences that you can't relate in words to a man," Adrienne says. "A woman knows immediately."

Mainly, when the daughters speak of friendship with men they describe camaraderie. "I guess my male friends are really buddies. They're not the friends I talk to about I how feel and what I'm going through," says Jennifer.

"It's always different talking to women than to men," Judith explains. "With men, it's not exactly just chitchat, but it's more about external than internal issues."

"I can be as close to men as to women when we talk about how it feels to go to the supermarket on a crowded day in New York City. But when it comes to your joys and your disappointments, those really intimate things, I've never met a man who can sustain those conversations," Adrienne says, sadly. "Deep down in their gut they don't know what I'm saying."

She concludes that "there's always something lacking between women and men"—even husbands. Linda discovers new meaning in her friendships with women as marriage and work swallow up her time and energy. "Now that we're paired off, it's hard to find time for each other. But we must. We're used to getting things from each other that our husbands can't give us. We *have* to keep our friendships going."

So what else is new? The books and articles written about how men evade, fumble, and botch intimate talk would line the equator if you laid them end to end. But it is not simply topics of conversation, or their absence, that characterize the daughters' friendships with men. Amy has a rich and complex relationship with a male coworker. They talk about relationships and family and all sorts of personal issues. They spend time together, apart from their spouses. In delicate political situations at work "Jack not only is supportive of me, but he also really understands the male-female element of the disputes and is very sympathetic." But Amy reveals that "I couldn't depend on him in my hour of need." When she was denied a promotion at work, Jack "avoided me, he just didn't talk to me. That's the way men deal with emotional issues. It's like they don't know what to say or how to act."

Renata makes friends more easily with men than with women. She enjoys and values her male friends, but admits that "the people who love me the most and whom I love—the people I trust—are women."

Ultimate trust and reliability—these words crop up repeatedly to describe the differences between the daughters' male and female friends. "I can talk about a lot of the same things with men as with women," says Rita. "But no, I don't have the same kinds of intimacy with men. See, my women friends are so *truly* and undoubtedly my friends. It doesn't matter if we fight or if they live halfway around the world from me. Our friendships are so permanent. It's not like that with men."

The daughters' bonds with women are not, however, one big love fest. Remember Mia's lament that "some women look at other women and tear them apart . . . to convince themselves that they're more attractive to men." Surely, she's speaking of the divisive rivalry that consciousness-raising aimed to replace with solidarity and love. So I query the daughters, as they are extolling female friendship, whether or how competition colors friendship—and competition over what?

Mia elaborates: "See, women are taught to think men are the prize. So women compete with each other instead of bonding. I feel it within myself." It is out there and it is within, that devil in the guise of competition with other women. The daughters feel it, and they struggle with it. Some of them simply surround themselves with women friends who refuse to engage in competition, especially over men. Like Renata: "A lot of women, foolish as it is, define themselves by how much men appreciate them. My friends and I, we don't get caught up in that. We're *friends*." Antonia confesses to an occasional twinge of jealousy, "but I don't allow it. I refuse to compete with another woman. I end up admiring the few women I've felt envious of. They're really great women, and I can totally see why a man would be interested in them, because they're so wonderful. You've got to bond with women."

Mary, an African American daughter, is justifiably proud of her accomplishments. She has worked hard to achieve her position as the administrator of a community social agency. Now, at thirty-five, she thinks hard about marriage—and about the competition. "So many women. You go to a bar or a café, tables full of women. A good-looking man comes in and everybody's thinking, who looks the best? Who's going to get him? There's a lot of us out there competing for men." The lament jars with Mary's many and varied expressions of female solidarity. So what does this do to sisterhood? "Not a thing," she says. "I won't have anything to do with that competition. I have a group of sisters, and I have *learned* not to be jealous or envious, and to give praise to any woman who has accomplished anything."

Yet even as they honor friendships between women, the daughters have a nagging sense that all is not as it should be. They imagine that their feminist mothers had an easier time forging strong bonds with other women. Jane envies her mother, who "got all the support she needed from other women. My mother says, 'Well, I just went out there and made it happen.' I tell my mother it's not like that these days. It's not so easy to say, 'Oh, let's form a group.' " It's the times, the daughters say. Jane feels that "these days everything is fragmented and scattered, people are so stressed about work or home life. I just get the feeling that there isn't the same kind of community there was twenty years ago."

Ingrid, too, is wistful. "I remember my mother's community. I don't see it happening now. It seems like everything is more individualized. If women came to me and said we're all going through the same experiences, let's get together and talk about them, I'd be happy to. But I can't go out and recruit women to do that."

Whatever is lacking in their female friendships, the daughters consciously seek out and cherish bonds with women—an unmistakable legacy of their mothers' feminism. And whatever is lacking in their friendships with men, the daughters are comfortable with men in ways that probably would have been unthinkable for their mothers. Men have become recognizable, demystified. Otherwise we would not find the camaraderie and real friendship that the daughters describe. To the extent that the workplace has become desegregated, incomplete as the process may be, the daughters mix with men as colleagues. In spite of the persistent sexual tension that gets in the way of "the making new of all relationships," friendship with men has something to do with the so-called sexual revolution.

Many feminists in the nineteenth and early twentieth centuries proposed to make women and men equal by imposing the same constraints on male sexual behavior as those that bound women: If it wasn't right for women, it wasn't right for men. Feminists of the sixties and seventies reversed the logic: If it's right for men, it's right for women. Away with the moralistic flimflam that sex is legitimate for women only if and when they marry, but natural and fun for men from the minute they are physiologically ready for it! This time, feminism advocated sexual freedom, not sexual shackles, for everyone; sex here, sex there, earlier sex, more sex, later sex, different sex, and—very important—enjoyable sex.

Every statistical survey reveals that women of the daughters' generation no longer defer their sexual lives until marriage. Adrienne Rich observes that women's freedom to have sex any old time "did not mean that we were free to discover our own sexuality, but rather that we were expected to behave according to male notions of female sexuality, as surely as any Victorian wife, though the notions themselves had changed." Yet, if the "notion" that women, like men, are entitled to sex when they want it falls significantly short of "discovering our own sexuality," it is nonetheless a notion that is unprecedented in our culture.

But if women in the world of my youth were bullied and shamed into preserving their virginity before marriage and their chastity after marriage, are the daughters similarly influenced by the prevailing mores to *have* sex? Has peer pressure simply been turned on its head?

"Probably," says Shanna, speaking of her adolescence. "But at that age you don't think of fancy concepts like peer pressure. It's just your world."

In the daughters' adolescent world, to become a

woman was not to menstruate, not to wear makeup, but to have sex. Renata was fifteen and still uninitiated when a girlfriend asked her whether she was a "woman" yet. "Even in high school I thought it was ridiculous to think of having sex as a rite of passage," Debby says. "But, like everyone else, I got sucked into it." Except for two daughters with a strong religious upbringing, the question for the daughters was not *whether* to have sex, but rather the fine points of *when*. The answer, in the adolescent years, depended somewhat on the mores of the larger community and, within it, the daughters' immediate social circles.

Adrienne moved from a conservative Catholic town on the East Coast to California when she was fourteen. Listening to her new girlfriends reminisce about sleeping with boys at the age of twelve and thirteen, "I was in a state of shock. Suddenly I was in California, and you were *supposed* to have sex. It got to be an enormous pressure. Finally, when I was an old lady—seventeen—I had sex."

Linda recalls that in the tenth grade of her Michigan high school, "this girl was celebrating the year's anniversary of when she lost her virginity. I looked at her like, whaaaaat? You lost your virginity *a year ago*? Of course, I didn't say it out loud. My friends didn't need to know I was still a virgin. But then, for me, it was a campaign to have sex as soon as possible."

"Oh, no, there was no pressure to have sex," Jenna confidently asserts. "I didn't—until the ninth grade. By then there was definitely pressure. Not to have sex just wasn't cool. It meant you weren't mature."

The few daughters who had no sexual experiences in high school thought of themselves as oddballs and outsiders. In the daughters' adolescent universe sexual relations were more than a sign of adulthood; they were an initiation into sisterhood. "You were excluded from a certain camaraderie among your girlfriends if you were still a virgin at a certain age," Heather wryly remarks. Rachel confesses that throughout the early years of high school she kept her virginity a secret. Her voice drops as if to dramatize her adolescent conspiracy with herself. "You just weren't cool. I remember feeling betrayed when my best friend announced that she was thinking about having sex. I felt that if she did, I had to." If their friends did not betray them, if the oddball group remained cohesive, these daughters cheerfully accepted their deviant status. But they were fully aware that by larger standards, in Jane's words, "you were a loser."

As we shall see, the imperative for adolescent males to collect sexual scalps has been untouched by the so-called sexual revolution. But the daughters seem surprised when I ask them whether they ever felt exploited by boys. Why should they? The daughters accept sex as their natural right, and most made the decision to have sex in a very deliberate way. "Exploited?" Nicole asks. "Not at all. I totally controlled the situation," she says of her first sexual experience at the age of sixteen.

The daughters learn to "control the situation" early in the formation of relationships with men. They don't wait to be chosen. They don't hover by the telephone, watching the clock and chewing their fingernails. Jenna is irritated with friends who criticize her for asking men out. "What are you supposed to do? Wait around to be picked and never do the picking yourself? I wasn't brought up to think that way."

Brenda makes overtures to men, but she admits that

"I'm a little bit nervous when I ask a guy out—as I'm sure men are. I wouldn't just go up to a really attractive man that I don't know and say, 'Let's go out to dinner.' After all, I'm offended when I think a man has asked me out just because he thinks I'm pretty. Once I know a guy, I do it in a more casual way. Nothing very formal. And it's not very formal when guys ask me out either."

"I have no problem asking a guy out—only the one that anyone has, fear of rejection," says Renata. "That has nothing to do with being a woman." Mary says, "It's a personality thing." She cannot bring herself to ask a man out because "I just can't take rejection. If I ask a man out and he isn't interested, I'm hurt." She envies friends for whom rejection "just rolls off their backs. No big deal, his loss." Only individual sensibilities, not taboos, deter the daughters of feminists from asking a man to dinner.

Ingrid recalls listening to her parents discuss a forthcoming vacation—Ingrid was fourteen—and "I decided right then and there I was going to lose my virginity before we went." Ingrid not only decided it was time to enter the sisterhood, she also announced the decision to her mother. "My mom said, 'I would prefer that you wait until you're seventeen, but it's OK.'" *She told her mother?* At the age of fourteen I could have sooner turned handsprings on the moon as tell my mother I was planning to have sex.

Soon after my daughter was born I began thinking about how, as a single *female* parent, I should order my sex life. Should I be open about it? Secretive? Something in between? As a feminist who (almost) took for granted my right to sexual pleasure with or without marriage, I wanted to convey to my daughter the same prerogative—without the "almost."

When my daughter was fifteen she asked for a dia-phragm. Together we went to our gynecologist and got one for her. That was easy. One evening a few months later she asked, out of the blue it seemed, whether her boyfriend Derek could spend the night. That was not so easy. My first impulse was to bellow "No!" I choked back the impulse and answered with a thoroughly fraud-ulent calm that I needed an hour to think about it. To myself I said, this is the time to put my money where my mouth is. Later that night she and Derek retired to her bedroom and I to mine. I didn't sleep all night. The next time was easier, and soon Derek's nocturnal presence was as natural as his presence at our dinner table had already been for several months.

Decisions about sexual behavior, one's own and one's daughter's, are private, intimate, and vastly more com-plex than public decisions about work, marriage, even "femininity." The feminist mothers' conflicts and dilem-mas about sex emerge filtered through the daughters' lens, and the picture is often blurred. Some parents looked more kindly on their sons' sexual awakening than their daughters'. The daughters who complained most about this double standard were children of "conven-tional" families.

The thorniest family conflict in Susanna's adolescence was provoked by her father's double standard. The boys in the family were accorded full latitude in their sexual shenanigans, while Susanna was forbidden "everything." The struggle appeared to be only with her father, because "he seemed to be laying down the rules." Now, at the age of thirty, Susanna realizes that her mother was com-plicit: "She was physically present, but she removed her-self, she'd be off in another world."

Adrienne's father, "old-fashioned and conservative,"

believed his daughter should keep sex on the back burner. While Adrienne's mother "made me feel it was something you could talk about, and we discussed sex a lot," she did it behind her husband's back.

Some of the daughters of single mothers *imagined* that without a father in the house, their mothers were more straightforward about sex. Amelia paraphrases her mother: " 'If you want to have sex, it's there for you and here's the birth control.' You see, there wasn't a father around in my life to say, 'You can't have sex until you get married.' " Perhaps it was easier for a single feminist mother to transmit to her daughter lessons on sexual equality. One could do it almost without words, simply by example. A single mother did not have to consult with a partner about this still-ticklish subject. Nor could she rely on a husband to play the heavy if she was less comfortable about a woman's equal right to sex than she would have preferred to admit.

Most of the daughters remember openly discussing sex and birth control with their mothers. When Amelia developed a close relationship with her first boyfriend at the age of fifteen, her mother insisted that Amelia get a diaphragm. "I said, 'Mom, I'm not interested in sex yet.' But she said, 'I still want you to have it. Just in case.' "

Some mothers told their daughters that sex without love leaves something to be desired, or that even in the presence of love, sex is not a simple business. Nicole is one of the few daughters to use the word *love* to describe her feelings about her first boyfriend. She was sixteen and "really wanted to have sex with him." Nicole's mother asked hard questions. "She told me that sex complicates a relationship. She told me to figure out for myself whether I needed to have sex with Robert."

The daughters believe that their feminist mothers were different from other mothers. Rita and her friends, all daughters of feminists, "knew about menstruation before any of the other girls did. We talked openly about sexuality, about pregnancy, disease, abortion. It came from our mothers. So when I had my first boyfriend, I felt fine, old enough."

Feminist mothers were neither handing out free tickets to sexual orgies nor secretly constructing emotional chastity belts. They struggled and waffled. But whatever they passed on by way of example or discussion or paraphernalia, their daughters are grateful, as Amelia puts it, that "my mom did not try to take sex away from me. When I was ready, I never had to sneak around."

Are there no boundaries, borders, rules in the daughters' new universe of sexual freedom? I remind the daughters how the mothers were expected to guard their virginity like a precious, nonrenewable resource, and to offer it up only in exchange for marriage. I tell them about Good Girls and Bad Girls ("damaged goods"). The daughters nod knowingly as I go through my spiel, only partly comprehending it. When I ask them about promiscuity, I sense that they are repressing an indulgent smile at a quaint, bookish word that only a mother might use. They use the word in our conversations, but only because I do. *Promiscuity* is too rigid a term to describe boundaries that are fluid and elusive, glimpsed out of the corner of the eye, never quite in sharp focus.

"I never did figure it out," Jane says thoughtfully. "In my circles there was a real fine line between being admired for having sex and being a slut. It was good to have sex, but not good to do it with a lot of guys." Rachel, too, was "pretty confused." She explains that the adolescent community is no less complex and varied than the adult world; "I had prissy, academic friends, an artsy-drama crowd, and my boyfriend was a rock band stoner. They all had different angles on sex. But in general, I guess it wasn't cool to have sex with too many people." Adrienne, telling me about a friend who has slept with forty-five men, says, "I guess I'm glad I haven't slept with tons of people. I've only slept with five." She does not consider herself to have been promiscuous. Her friend? Well, perhaps a bit "easy."

On the face of it, then, promiscuity is a numbers game. Some partners, OK. Too many, not OK. But what does "too many" mean?

The daughters are not really talking about numbers. "We had certain standards," Adrienne insists, "although to the outsider it would've looked pretty casual. The girls who were called sluts—we said, 'Oh man, she'll sleep with anyone.' I guess it meant a girl who slept with one person one week, another the next week. The girls who weren't promiscuous slept with guys they liked." As Luz puts it, the slut was the girl who "slept around." But "it was fine if you slept with your boyfriend."

In the daughters' adolescent world serial monogamy was "fine," sexual dalliances were suspect. They are shy about using the word *love,* as if it were inappropriate for an adolescent, and they use a number of less extravagant synonyms. Adrienne is glad that her first sexual experience was with "a person that I liked." Other daughters speak about the difference between promiscuity and acceptable sexual behavior in terms of "caring about" the partner. If sex took place within a relationship that "meant something," the girl was not promiscuous, numbers notwithstanding.

I ask the daughters whether boys and girls were judged the same way. Was it equally unacceptable for boys to sleep around with girls they didn't care about?

"You mean a double standard?" Cary asks, her tone implying that I might as well come straight out with it. "There were totally different standards. *Totally*. About a guy, they'd say he gets around, about a girl they'd say she's a slut."

Like the drone of bagpipes, the same monotonous note sounds through every daughter's narrative. The girl was a slut, the boy was cool; a boy might change his ways and be forgiven, a girl was marked for the duration of her adolescence. Yet there is something written between the lines of this tired old story: The daughters of feminists were uneasy collaborators in this morality tale. "We talked about it all the time," Jenna recalls. "Why are girls called sluts? Why are guys who sleep around called cool? It didn't make any sense to us."

It made no sense to the daughters of feminists, schooled in equality, because "the girl was a slut and the boy was cool" was not a universal verdict. It depended— not entirely, but mainly—on who was doing the judging. Becky mentions her older brother. "Knowing him and all his friends, I was always aware that people definitely looked down on girls who slept around, but not on boys." Midsentence, she has shifted from the masculine pronoun—"Knowing *him* and all his friends"—to the collective noun, *people*. So, who's doing the judging? Renata translates: "Sure, there was a double standard. Among *men*, a woman who sleeps around is a slut, but a guy is cool. Among women, it isn't like that. Women have no respect for a guy like that."

The daughters were, or were trying to be, evenhanded.

Anyone, male or female, who pursues sex indiscriminately, a qualitative rather than a quantitative judgment, is unworthy of respect—or, as Shanna expresses it, "untrustworthy." The double standard did not mean one kind of acceptable behavior for men and another for women. It meant two distinct judgments, male and female.

Ingrid puts it bluntly. "That tag—slut—it doesn't come from women, it comes from men. From women, it's not a judgment, it's concern. If one of my friends is sleeping with a lot of different men, I'm not judging her, I'm worried about her because of diseases."

Moreover, the female definition of promiscuity often had more to do with sexual "come on" than sexual behavior. Ingrid, an "ugly duckling" in junior high school, was very popular in high school. "Suddenly I had all these different boyfriends. I'd get tired of each of them in two weeks, but I was having such a wonderful time. It was totally innocent. We walked around together, I wore his jacket. No sex." On her first day of high school, she was shocked to find *Ingrid Andersen Is a Slut* scribbled on the wall of the girls' bathroom. It still surprises her. "It was so weird, because I was a virgin."

Rita agrees that "it had almost nothing to do with actual sexual behavior. At my school you were considered a slut if you wore tons of makeup and really tight clothes and flirted a lot at lunchtime."

"To be honest," Linda confesses, "the girls we called sluts weren't doing anything that we weren't doing. But they came on to boys more provocatively."

Some daughters considered a girl promiscuous who "acted like the guys were more important." As Linda explains, "There was an unspoken pact; you would never put a guy before your girlfriends. So a girl who gave up her girlfriends for a guy? Forget her! She's promiscuous. A slut."

The daughters I interviewed have navigated the rough waters of their adolescent years and put into the calmer, if not safer, port of young adulthood. With maturity, the daughters have become more generous—to themselves as well as to their sisters. They do not consider casual sex a criterion for judging anyone's character.

"It can be fun to have a lot of sexual and romantic experiences. I've enjoyed it at times," says Judith, twenty-seven, matter-of-factly. "I have many friends who have a lot of relationships with a lot of different people. I would never think of them as promiscuous."

Ingrid mulls over varieties of sexual relationships. "Friends who are lonely and decide to sleep together— that's fine. Or if you go to a party and meet someone that turns you on, that's all right too."

"To me, promiscuity only means not being candid," says Lola. "If you're straightforward with your partner and say, 'Well, I'm planning to have sex with several people and you're one of them—how do you feel about it?' then it's not promiscuity."

Paradoxically, many daughters feel they have grown more conservative over time. A contemplative approach has replaced the crackle and electricity of adolescent sexual exploration, the feverish haste to become a sexual being. "Sometimes I look back on those days and I think I was too promiscuous," Linda says. "I should have known that sex wasn't the key to happiness." Grace believes that "there's nothing wrong with casual sex—it just isn't good enough."

Susan, who spent ten years in a commune, describes

herself in those years as "quite promiscuous. I had this idea that we should all be each others' sexual partners." She has no regrets; in fact, she finds it all pretty funny in retrospect. But now, she says with a laugh, "I can't imagine having affairs with everyone. It's too much work. It's like a full-time job. I'd never get anything done."

Nina is relieved that she is no longer driven to seek out sexual adventures because "then it was like I wasn't really somebody unless I was with a guy." Looking back to that time, she says, "I can hardly believe it. I don't know where that came from." She smiles. "I know it didn't come from my mother. My mother tried to teach me that relationships aren't the way to make yourself happy. Once you're happy with yourself, then you can seek a relationship."

To say that the daughters have grown more conservative is another way of saying more careful. Pregnancy, the mothers' bugaboo, scarcely rates a mention. AIDS, the most menacing of all constraints on sexual freedom, everybody's sexual freedom, has replaced pregnancy as the wages of—what? Not, as it turns out, of sin.

When I ask Lola whether as an adult she has a definition of promiscuity, she answers, "Not really. But I have a definition of stupidity." For her, stupidity is sex without condoms. Nicole, bringing up the subject of AIDS, flatly states, "If I'm with a guy who is sleeping around, the sexual part of the relationship is over for me." She tells me about a close friend who made love to a man she had just met. "I was incensed when she said they hadn't used a condom. I yelled at her, 'How could you be so *stupid?*' I'm so pissed off at women who don't think enough of themselves to say to a guy, 'Do you think you could use a rubber, please?'"

The risk of disease is the daughters' spontaneous response to the query about how, as adults, they regard promiscuity. Stupidity—carelessness—defines unseemly sexual behavior. The daughters are pragmatic, not moralistic. They have broken the connection between sex and its erstwhile accomplices, sin and guilt.

In the daughters' sexual calculus yet another concern vies for importance with health risks. Judith, for whom varied sexual experiences are fun and exciting, admits, "If I had a friend who was sleeping around, I'd be concerned—and not just about AIDS. I'd be concerned about her emotional health."

"Why are you sleeping around?" Rachel would ask of such a friend. "What are you looking for?" She emphasizes that this isn't about morals. "It's about psychological health."

"Promiscuity means something different to me now than when I was a kid," Shanna says. "Women—and men, too—who sleep around, they seem to need reassurance all the time. I check myself to see that I'm not doing that. It's not a moral issue. I just don't ever want to feel that I need the sexual attention of men to make me happy."

The daughters insist that they question the emotional wisdom of random sexual behavior equally for men and women, but they make enough little slips of the tongue to suggest that their impartiality is more a wish than a fact. Amelia describes a friend's behavior. "She goes out with a guy once, and the next time, she sleeps with him. And she can be sleeping with four or five guys in the same week. To me that's worse than promiscuous." This friend, Amelia concludes, has no respect for her body. I ask her whether she judges men who behave as her friend does the same way.

"Yeah, I do," she says quickly. Then, almost in the same breath, she changes her mind. "No. I don't." She laughs self-consciously and clears her throat. "I think that when women are promiscuous, they're using sex to feel good about themselves. For men, it's more of a game, a game with their male friends. It's a power thing. Because men sort of have the power already. It's given to them at birth. That's the way it is, unfortunately, in our society." She hesitates, groping for words. "Women use it as a way to get some sort of security and confidence that they can't get on their own and that they can't get from other women. That's a problem for women who don't have feminist mothers. They depend on a man to make them feel good."

Everybody talks about the changes in women's sexual behavior as a sexual revolution. I do it, too. I find myself thinking of the sexual universe of the bad old days as the *status quo ante bellum* and of the feminist mothers as the theoreticians, strategists, and infantry of the battles for sexual liberation. But my conversations with the daughters of feminists suggest that the metaphor of revolution is both inflated and skewed. Boys and men still have an arsenal of nasty names for girls and women who "sleep around," but, in Jane's words, "when guys sleep around, they're proud. Can you imagine—it's still called 'scoring'?" That's only half a revolution. But that "most girls and women no longer accept such labeling without question or contention," as Lillian Rubin points out in her book *Erotic Wars*, "is one of the unheralded gains of the feminist movement."

A concern with women's sexuality was an inevitable corollary of the feminist movement, as it had been of all women's movements in the past. But the mothers' generation of feminists was lucky; it had a little help from technology. The power to avoid pregnancy, and that power held in one's own hands, was a gift, a bonanza. With or without the women's movement, developments in birth control would have changed sexual behavior, but not necessarily morality. I can easily imagine women with the ability to avoid pregnancy *still* feeling guilty, immoral, slutty about having sex without marriage, although they might have done it anyway. I can easily imagine women, unconstrained by "morality" in the timing of their sex, *still* feeling shame, or even ignorance, over their own definitions of pleasurable sex.

It was the women's movement that guided and shaped the consequences of technology, that enabled women to imagine having sex without guilt *and* to think about discovering our own sexuality, however murky the goal may yet be. As Barbara Ehrenreich and Deirdre English have demonstrated, "evidence of the primary role of the clitoris in female sexuality had never been lacking." It was not technology, but the women's movement, that empowered "women . . . to speak up for their subjective sexual experience as a *fact*, not a neurosis."

One day my daughter, at the ripe old age of ten, said that the kids at school had been talking about oral sex and asked me what it was. I told her. Eyes round and mouth gaping, she demanded, "Do you do that?" Having long since vowed to honestly answer her questions, sexual or otherwise, I answered (gulp) yes. Drawing herself up, she announced, "Well, I think that's completely disgusting," and marched off to her room. Knowing my daughter-the-adult, I can say without the slightest hesitation that her childish censure evolved into adult sexuality with an ease that can only astonish and delight my generation. The women's movement can take the credit for my honesty and for the benefits that my daughter reaped.

I must confess that I did not feel as free to probe into the daughters' subjective sexual experience, into what gives them pleasure and how they seek it, as I do with my own daughter. I have not yet shaken the dust from my boots on the long journey from my prefeminist days. Perhaps someday a daughter of a feminist, less diffident than I, will write a book that more fully explores the consequences of the feminists' quest for their own sexuality. But the daughters often volunteered answers to questions only implied.

"My mother was always open with me about sex," says Nicole. "We had these really beautiful talks about women's sexual organs and women's sexuality." Now, she says, although "I still have so many emotional things about sex, I confront a man in bed with my feelings even if I go all red in the face. And I won't do anything in bed that makes me uncomfortable."

Antonia, searching for her own sexuality, can say that "the funny thing is that I could see myself in a relationship with a woman, although I've never had one. But I have this feeling that people are just people, and it doesn't feel weird to think about it even if it never happens."

Olivia, a lesbian daughter, attributes her courage in exploring her sexuality to her mother's defiance of convention, "which she did simply by being a feminist. She encouraged me to be my own person, an individual—preferably, not a straight homemaker or secretary."

Discussing pornography, Heather says it is not the thing itself that she objects to but that most pornography "panders only to male fantasies." "Why can't we all have our fantasies pandered to?" she asks.

Ellie and Jenna, twenty-four and twenty-one respectively, have put behind them periods of heavy sexual activity. For the moment, both have chosen to be celibate. "I just want to be celibate for a time, to sit back and think about what sex means to me," Ellie says.

Naomi Wolf, author of *The Beauty Myth* and a feminist of the daughters' generation, is probably reflecting her wish more than reality when she says that "love freely given between equals is the child of the women's movement." As Debby points out, "the power is still there for men in sexual relations. And they even manipulate feminism to keep it. Men have said to me—why won't you sleep with me, aren't you a liberated woman? And I say, 'I won't sleep with you *because* I'm a liberated woman, and I do what I want to do.'"

The feminist mothers, guiding and shaping the course of sexual liberation, achieved only half a revolution, but it is the half that the daughters can control. That, it seems to me, is a pretty good place to start discovering our own sexuality and even to begin reshaping all relationships.

CHAPTER SIX
. . . .

Would You Want Your Mother's Life?

> *Family likeness has often a deep sadness in it.*
> *Nature, that great tragic dramatist, knits us*
> *together, by bone and muscle, and divides us by the*
> *subtler web of brain; blends yearning and*
> *repulsion; and ties us by our heartstrings to the*
> *beings that jar us at every movement.*
>
> **—GEORGE ELIOT, *ADAM BEDE*, 1859**

Just before I conducted the first interview for this book I decided to do a trial run with my daughter Evie to refine the questions I was devising for the daughters of other feminists. The misbegotten event took place in a house that Evie had never inhabited, in a city far from her birthplace. But it felt like old times because we sat at the battered kitchen table that I had acquired in 1970 when Evie was six years old and carted from apartment to apartment, from California to New York and back again. Every meal my daughter and

136

I ate together until she left home at eighteen was eaten at that table.

Evie is forthright—to a fault, some might say when she blasts forth opinions better hedged or even left unspoken. She is not shy about shouting me down on the feminist issues over which we disagree. But, in a fit of daughterly indulgence, she tried to give me the answers she knew I hoped for. Caught between her desire to please me and her desire to hold her ground, she chafed. I assured her, as I would later tell the daughters of other feminists, that there are no "right" answers. She couldn't quite believe me. Just as our mutual irritation approached the boiling point, we looked at each other and burst out laughing. The "interview" was over. The undercurrent in our conversation, of course, was not this or that issue, but twenty-some years of living together in love, antagonism, and authority challenged.

To state the obvious, there is more to the relationship between daughters of feminists and their mothers than the mothers' feminism. If I didn't know it before, I certainly knew it after that attempt to interview my daughter. But when I interviewed the daughters of feminists, I did not intend to probe into the emotional/psychological maelstrom of mother-daughter relationships. For one thing, the vast literature that attempts to sort out this relationship assumes that there is something innate, predetermined, and universal in the relationship between mother and daughter. To paraphrase Suzanna Danuta Walters in her book *Lives Together/Worlds Apart,* the study of mother-daughter relationships is mainly confined to psychological description and prescription, too little located "in the more varied realm of culture and society." In other words, this literature is too little aware of how the mother-daughter relationship, as perhaps all others, is imbedded in the historical moment. It is not helpful to someone who is trying to sort out the differences between one historical moment and another.

But try as I might to stay on solid ground, the daughters themselves led me into the quicksand. The daughters *wanted* to embellish their responses to their mothers' feminism with flashes of insight on the emotional dimension of their relationships. And they wanted to know from me whether other daughters of feminists have the kind of relationships that they have with their mothers.

In the early days of the women's movement I had an illuminating conversation with a student of mine. The student told me that she was in a bad mood because after graduation she was planning to move back to her hometown. Perplexed, I asked what was so terrible about that. "I'm moving back home because I miss my mother. All my friends are treating me like a pariah," she answered grimly.

That was 1972, and the student was violating a taboo accepted as such by my generation, which, for better or worse, was hell-bent on questioning traditional homilies of filial piety. Aided by the trickle-down of poorly digested Freudian theory and its poisonous offshoots, like Philip Wylie's "momism," many young women of my generation blamed Mom for everything. To be different from one's mother, to be misunderstood and to feel stifled by her, proved that one was appropriately "individuating." We took the process to be a law of nature. We protofeminists believed that it was impossible to be intimate with our mothers because they had nothing better to do with their lives than to stifle us. It took a long time and a lot of feminism to transform scorn first into understanding and then into compassion for our mothers, not only as mothers but as women of their times.

Although the popular media and scholarship still traffic in these ideas about mothers' destructive influences, only the muted echo of their once robust roar reaches the ears of the daughters of feminists. I interview Susan almost twenty years after the conversation with my student. Turning popular assumptions upside down, Susan asks, "Isn't there a theory that feminist mothers are more fulfilled and don't live as much through their children as other mothers? And that they value their daughters more than nonfeminist mothers?" She assumes that daughters of feminists have better relationships with their mothers than "other daughters."

Susan and her mother have had their ups and downs, "especially when I was an adolescent. I wanted to be out on the street taking drugs and having fun. Somehow my mother didn't think it was such a great idea." Nonetheless, Susan says, "I feel so close to my mother, and I always have, even in the bad times when I was growing up." She wants to know if her own experience is common to all daughters of feminists.

Flick the kaleidoscope and the pieces fall into every pattern of ambivalence between feminist mothers and their daughters that besets any truly intimate relationship. At some point in their lives—often (but not always) in adolescence—the daughters learned how to vex their mothers. A few daughters did it with drama and near tragedy. Cynthia ran away from home at age fourteen to marry an abusive, tyrannical man (from whom she is now divorced). I ask, "What was in your head when you ran away?" Cynthia answers, "I wanted to get back at my mother. She hurt me so much, I thought now it's my turn. What I did was to hurt myself, but I guess everybody learns the hard way."

Nina did drugs and "totally blew it" at school. "It was all about power," she says. Challenging her mother's authority "was my job in life. It was like I was saying, "Power? Oh yeah? Well, watch *this!*" "

Most daughters played out gentler variations on this theme.

"When I got into adolescence, well, if she said up, I said down," Lola says, laughing. "Mainly, I felt like I wasn't getting the perks commensurate with my responsibilities around the house."

In adolescence Antonia had "really terrible fights" with her mother. Now she puts the fights into the context of family politics and her position as the third of five children, all clamoring for attention. She can't even remember what the fights were about.

Becky describes her rebellious stage: "I was, well, rambunctious and I went out more than my mother would have liked. But I never rebelled against her beliefs. I always really understood and respected them."

Some daughters unerringly let their darts fly at their mothers' feminist values. "Some kids rebelled by doing drugs. I rebelled by joining a sorority and being a cheerleader," Nicole says, stifling a giggle.

"My mom was always preaching." Olivia rolls her eyes. " 'Don't shave your legs! Don't shave your armpits! Don't wear makeup!' So I went through a phase where I did all those things because she didn't want me to. Now I don't do any of that."

"According to my mother I started rebelling when I was eleven and didn't stop until I was nineteen," Adrienne says. "I did it by pushing her values to the limit rather than by rejecting them." She characterizes her mother's way of transmitting feminist principles as " 'don't do as I *do*; do as I *say*.' I heard what she said, all right. I think all daughters hear what their mothers say. I thought, 'You want a free spirit? I'll give you a free spirit!' I gave her more than she bargained for."

For some daughters the mutinous eye opens only in adulthood and, in a few cases, then perceives the mother's feminist convictions as excesses. One daughter—I will call this daughter X because she asked me to—regards her mother's persistent activism as inappropriate for a woman in her fifties. Her mother is "still" a community activist in feminist organizations at the expense of a "real job." "My sister and brother and I laugh about it, but we say it's time for her to grow up."

Amanda sees her mother as a modern female Don Quixote who vainly tilts at windmills. She illustrates with the story of her mother's tenacious but unsuccessful fight for tenure at a major university. "My mom's very smart and she has incredible credentials, a Ph.D and a law degree. And more training and experience and publications than some of those old conservative men that were denying her tenure." Amanda believes that her mother "should have just walked away from that conflict. She yelled and screamed and nothing happened. She put all her energy into seeing nothing happen." Worse, in Amanda's estimation, her mother failed to profit from her failure, for she continues to be caught up "in the next great feminist idea, the next battle." Her mother, Amanda believes, does not "take care of herself."

Most of the daughters who criticize their mothers' feminism come at it from the opposite direction and chide their mothers for feminist shortcomings. Olivia, twenty-four, says, "My mother has done amazing things. My mother was like a goddess to me, a deity. Powerful, nothing could stop her. Now I look at her, and she's just a human being. I can't believe that I'm sometimes so angry at her for not doing *more*."

Another daughter gets "really mad" at her mother because "she falls apart when my father goes out of town. She's scared to be in the house by herself. Here's this woman who is so strong in so many ways. Why is she so dependent?"

Rachel, too, is disappointed with her mother for falling short of the ideal. "One thing that really bugs me is that she always expects my father to take care of all the physical things in life. And I was always being told that was sexist." Rachel wonders whether that has influenced her own choice to work as a gardener.

Debby finds her mother's self-effacement irritating. "My mom is absolutely as smart as my father, but she refuses to see it that way." Debby believes that her mother "doesn't really understand how patriarchal this society is."

Each daughter has her own rhythm and timing in her relationship with her mother, each her own critical twist. But they all seem to be unaware of the imperative of the mothers' generation to wrench themselves from their mothers' stifling ministrations. "There was a time when we didn't get along," says Marcia. "But we're very close now. Sometimes when I'm talking to her I forget she's my mother, because she's really a friend."

Luz reminisces about the bad times. "We've had spats and didn't speak to each other for weeks." Now, she says, "we have the kind of relationship I'd like to have with my own child. We're so open with each other, and so close."

In her last year of high school and first year of college Maureen, now twenty-two, was "wild, rebellious, and alcoholic." She was furious with her siblings, her absentee father, and especially her mother. "Now I'm very, very close to her. I can talk to her about anything. She's always there for me. She's not judgmental, and she doesn't get angry if we disagree."

Adrienne says, "My mother always made me feel like I was really special and that I could do things she wasn't able to do. I'm really grateful for that. We're very close."

I can't be sure that the touching intimacy between the daughters of feminists and their mothers derives in some linear fashion from their mothers' feminism, mainly because I did not interview daughters of women who are not feminists. Nor can I say that the determining factor in these relationships is the mothers' personal fulfillment in the world of work in addition to motherhood. I can't even be sure that the way the mothers supported and encouraged their daughters as *women* fostered the intimacy. But it is certainly tempting to speculate that the characteristics of mothers who are proud to be women, and proud to be the mothers of daughters, are tightly woven into this fundamental and dynamic relationship.

Describing the intimacy that they enjoy with their mothers, some daughters say it dates back to their earliest sentient days. For others, intimacy has developed only recently. With the passage of time, the few who continue to feel distant from their mothers may grow closer to them. But all the daughters, immersed in their mothers' history, some of which they have seen unfold before their very eyes, are proud and admiring.

Listen to daughter *X*, who casts such a bleak eye on her mother's unflagging feminist activism. "The funny thing is that I'm so proud of her in many ways. I'll meet people and they'll say, 'I know this woman, she's been such an inspiration for me, she's so wonderful.' And I go, oh my God, they're talking about my mother. She hangs in there and still has the passion for it, and people admire her. And, you know, I admire her too. I'm very proud. But I'd like to see her reap the benefits."

"She's an incredible woman," Nina says of her mother, a labor lawyer well known in her community. "She's strong and dynamic and motivated to do lots of things, not just one thing. She's definitely a great role model, as a single female—or just as a woman in this world who stands on her own two feet."

Becky talks about her mother's career as a community college teacher and her pursuit of a doctorate late in her forties, about her unrelenting political involvements. "I was always proud of my mother and impressed with what she could do, being a single parent and a feminist and having these incredible beliefs and doing all these things. And her activism. When she believes in something, she just goes out and works on it." Above all, Becky values her mother for "doing something that goes beyond equal rights. It's more that she's a model of a woman who can be entirely independent."

Cynthia saw her mother "for so many years going to school, going to work, taking care of us kids. Now she's independent. She has a good job and she's involved in so many things." Cynthia also saw her mother in a relationship with a man who "abused her physically and made her cry all the time. He was driving her crazy. Now she wouldn't stand for that kind of stuff. That's what I love and admire about her. She's so tough." When Cynthia hits a hard patch in her own life, "I look at myself and then I look at my mother, and I understand that I'm letting myself down." She draws on her mother's example for nourishment.

"My mother is such a strong role model," says Ellie. "I feel really lucky that she is such a committed feminist. I feel really lucky that she's always supported and valued me. I'm doing what I want to do and being what I want to be, and it has to do with her."

I hesitate to call what the daughters express about their mothers "heroine worship." That would reduce each vibrant, complex, polychromatic canvas to a monochromatic still life. But even on those canvases on which the yellow of jaundice peeps here and there through other hues, the figure of the mothers is large and impressive.

This is not the overwrought figure of the mom from whose tentacles the daughter must disengage, whom at all costs she must not emulate. For the daughters of feminists, the mothers are examples of what women can and should be.

It seemed logical to me, therefore, to ask the daughters whether the world would be a better place if women ran it. The way I phrase the question violates one of the cardinal rules of interviewing: Never ask a question that can be answered by a simple yes or no. And, indeed, as if I had tapped their knees with a rubber mallet the daughters throw out a reflexive yes or no. But not a single daughter is satisfied with her monosyllable and, unbidden, spins off into the complexities hidden in the question's apparent simplicity.

"This is a conversation my friends and I have a lot of fun with," Renata says. "We come up with these great imaginary worlds run by women. So I'd say, let's try it!" Then Renata switches from science fiction to realism.

"But I don't know how different it would be from the world we have now." She is not enchanted by the few female leaders on a world scale that come to mind. "I'd like to think that women would deal differently with problems like militarism, imperialism, and war. But there you have Thatcher and Gandhi. Then again," she says wishfully, "with women in power all over the place, people wouldn't be socialized that way."

Like many of the daughters, Jennifer believes that giving women the power to run the show would not guarantee improvement because "we come from the same place, we live in the same world as men do. We've learned a lot of the same things."

Susan believes that "all kinds of things make one a good person, not just being a woman. Generally men do more evil because they have more power. It's pretty romantic to think women are purer and better."

"I would never vote for a woman just because she's a woman," Olivia states. "Not if she has bad values, like racism and homophobia, not if she doesn't care about homelessness and hatred and corruption."

Anne-Marie notices that "in a sexist society people look more carefully at a woman's record than a man's. I really worry about that. God, it scares me that there are so few women in leadership positions. Would the world be better if there were more? Depends on which women." Anne-Marie's idea of the kind of woman not to vote for is Margaret Thatcher. "More progressive women—not just women. I'd get behind that. But I'd have to support their politics, just like with men."

In Ellie's opinion, a mirror image of what already exists is just a bad reflection of a bad situation: "A lot of my friends think that women should just take over the world and totally subject men to sexism. I think that's really dumb." On the other hand, she muses, "maybe it would be a better world. Women are taught to listen and to make compromises. They're more interested in solving problems than in making a show of power." Then the ubiquitous anti-icons of female power, Margaret Thatcher and Indira Gandhi, spring to mind. "I just don't understand these women," says Ellie. "I guess they relinquish the use they could put their power to in exchange for male support."

It scarcely matters where the daughters begin; they end up in the same place. Hilary's first response to the question is as adamant a yes as Ellie's no. "Definitely!" says Hilary. "Women have borne the brunt of our economic and social policies. In that realm they have the ability to understand what's needed better than men." For Hilary, women like Thatcher are irrelevant examples, because as things stand now, "the only women who get through are the women that the men allow to get through." They are the ones that, as Ellie puts it, "are either puppets of men or think they have to play the conservative game. They betray women." Hilary agrees with Ellie that "women alone have to fit into an existing structure that they have not set up. If, for example, the House and Senate were half female, women would be working with other women."

"Of course the world would be better if women ran it," Lola says. "That's not even up for discussion. Good Lord! Can you imagine giving birth to a child and sending that child to war?" She swerves for a moment when I bring up Thatcher and Gandhi. "Well, I guess that while the cream rises, the shit floats. But if women had an equal chance at the starting gate, things would be different."

Amelia laughs at the question. "Definitely!" she answers. "I hate to say it, but yes, I do, I do. I think we're stronger, nicer. We're sensitive, more in tune because we're the ones with children growing inside of us." Amelia believes that women like Thatcher and Gandhi were born in the "old country." Such women rise in the leaven of male-dominated society. "If conditions were different, we wouldn't have to let go of our sensitivities when we get power."

If the daughters waffle a bit on either side of the question, they agree—they hope—that the world would be a better place if world leaders had qualities *defined* as feminine. Looking at the evidence, they agree that individual women may not have these qualities; that women in the aggregate do; that until women in the aggregate, or men like them, have "an equal chance at the starting gate," the world will lumber on much as it has.

Embedded in the question about whether the world would be a better place if women had more power is an issue fundamental to understanding how the daughters of feminists think about sex and gender; an issue that persistently engages feminist and antifeminist alike; an issue that entraps and creates false dichotomies because it asks the wrong question. Precisely because that wrong question is part of our cultural public discourse, I ask it too: Do perceived differences between men and women result from nature or nurture, from biological imperatives or socialization?

In the nature/nurture controversy the daughters fall squarely into the nurture camp. How could it be otherwise for these women, so acutely conscious that their mothers defied biological "destiny," making themselves into something they weren't supposed to be? And it cuts both ways: The daughters reject biological determinism as an explanation for both women's virtues and men's failings.

"To tell the truth," Christine says, "I think men and women have the same characteristics. But some of the characteristics are suppressed in men and some in women. I have male friends who are sensitive, but they're not allowed to show it."

Ellie rejects the notion that a world dominated by women would be better because "when people say things like that they're arguing for innate differences between men and women. I can't *abide* biological arguments."

"Maybe there's something to men being a little more aggressive because of testosterone—or something to a woman's maternal instincts," Brenda says. "But I have friends who discourage the macho jerk syndrome in their little boys. The little boys are socialized to be *not* aggressive. And it works! It's socialization."

While a few of the daughters toy with the idea that childbearing carries with it some special qualities, for most, like Brenda, nature/nurture is a secular issue. The daughters are indifferent to replacing the male gods of contemporary established religions with goddesses, real or imagined, culled from prehistoric reconstructions. They are singularly uninterested in devising new rituals to commemorate the goddess within or without. It is the same secular spirit that leads them to reject mythologized biology as well.

The daughters, arguing for the greater importance of socialization, are not dismissing biology. It never seems to occur to them to argue that human beings are born a blank slate. Without the slightest hesitation or defensiveness they assert that men are by nature physically stronger than women—or, at least, most men are stronger than most women. But what, they ask, does that have to do with behavior and attitudes, not to speak of rewards?

Stephen Jay Gould, pondering the argument that the human race is innately aggressive, points to a particular culture that was warlike and aggressive at one historical stage and is now tranquil and unaggressive: "If some peoples are peaceable now, then aggression cannot be encoded in our genes, only the potential for it. If innate only means possible, or even likely in certain environments, then everything we do is innate and the word has no meaning."

Susan, like the other daughters, says the same thing in her own way: "There's no way to tell now whether behavior is genetic. It's all so covered up by socialization." She stops to think. "Well, let's say there are genetic differences. But when people say that because something is genetic it's immutable, that's bullshit. It can be changed even if it is genetic. Certainly it's not genetic that men make more money than women."

I ask the daughters "Would you want your mother's life?" The question is barely out of my mouth before the majority of the daughters answer "No!" These daughters who so admire their mothers' achievements look on their mothers' lives as an unrelieved obstacle course. Amelia explains that "I admire my mother so much. She's very intelligent, very successful. She's a powerful woman. I'm proud of her and I love her deeply. She's done a lot, a whole lot, and people know her name. I can imagine that for myself." But for Amelia's taste her mother has had to "climb too many mountains." "She grew up in a traditional family. She knew the man she was going to marry even before she went to college, and the only reason she went to college was that in her Ivy League family it was the thing to do. I wouldn't want that."

"My mother had to work against such oppressive factors," says Renata. "She came from a family where she would be working really hard, studying, and her father would interrupt and demand that she make him a sandwich. She had to deal with all that."

"When my mother was a child," says Jenna, "in her Jewish family she wasn't even considered a person because she was female. I wouldn't want to have to fight against that."

Liza says with compassion that "my mother wasn't raised to question injustice against women, the way I was. She had to fight her family all the way—and the whole society."

Looming large on the daughters' list of their mothers' hardships are early marriage and early motherhood—or, as the daughters see it, premature marriage and untimely motherhood. Judith, twenty-seven, is appalled to think that at her age her mother was already married and had a two-year-old child. "I think that because she married so early there were parts of herself that were submerged. I hope that the parts of myself come out before I make that huge decision."

Ellie, reviewing her mother's youth, shudders visibly. "When my mother talks about the expectations for women when she was my age in the fifties and the kinds of things she worried about—wow! She says you were really an old maid if you didn't get married. That seems like light-years away."

Heather's mother married at age twenty-nine, late by

the standards of those days. "But, you know, she lived at home when she was in college, then she lived with her sister, and then she got married and lived with my dad." Heather lives alone and loves it. "It just wasn't socially acceptable when she was young. I'd have hated that."

"Not for me, her life," Olivia says firmly. "I'd never get married and have a kid in my early twenties. I could never do what society thinks I'm *supposed* to do.

Hilary's mother "did things and accepted things that I'd hate to have to deal with. Like getting married and having kids at twenty because that's what every woman was supposed to do."

The daughters perceive that even when their mothers did "what every woman was supposed to do," their very compliance was turned against them. Laurie's mother, now a successful academic, became pregnant in graduate school. Her dissertation supervisor insisted that she have an illegal abortion and generously found her a doctor who would perform one. He took her refusal as a betrayal. Judith, a law student, talks about how the "white male establishment held my mother down. When I was born her university told her not to come back. They said now that you have a baby, you don't need to finish your doctorate. She had to work too hard to get the academic recognition she deserves. I have it much easier. It's not that I don't like to work, but I don't want to work that hard."

As we have seen, the daughters' fantasies do not include amassing fortunes. At the same time, the daughters, especially but not exclusively the daughters of mother families, often single out their mothers' economic struggles as the one they would most like to avoid.

Maureen's voice trembles when she tells me that "it

was no fun watching my mom trying to deal with six kids on her own when my father's checks were always late and she had to worry about groceries." Anne-Marie's mother, having done a stint as a struggling single parent, was not relieved of complete economic responsibility for her family after she remarried. "Her husband is . . . well." Anne-Marie shrugs. "She was still stuck pulling for all of us. I don't want those economic pressures."

The daughters often make a clear distinction between their mothers' professional and personal quandaries, a distinction the mothers might not have made. "I'm so impressed by all the struggling, all the hard work she's had to do. She's done so much for herself *by* herself, and she's so strong. I really respect that," Luz says of her mother's professional achievements. "But I've seen her lose herself. She was with a guy for five years who left her for a woman my age. It tore her up for two years. I don't want that."

The most important lesson Ingrid has learned from her mother's life is that "women should not allow themselves to be in oppressive relationships. My mom and I were talking last night and she agreed that a feminist is someone who's not in a destructive, oppressive relationship like she was in for twelve years."

Renata would "definitely want some parts" of her mother's life—"She has a good head on her shoulders, she's productive, and she devotes her energies in good ways"—but she doesn't think her mother has done very well in her "personal relationships with men." Witness to her mother's "furious wars with my father over egalitarian sharing of duties and work," Renata doesn't think much better of the men in her mother's life since the divorce. "They were never her equal. To be in an oppressive relationship is a contradiction of everything a feminist preaches. You should never, *ever* allow yourself to be in an oppressive relationship." Then, with a sigh, Renata adds, "But I guess you can love someone who isn't necessarily good for you."

The "personal" is not just a matter of relationships. Some mothers also sacrificed other good things that the daughters don't wish to relinquish. "My mother's had a really wonderful life and I respect and admire it. But I think that she's been so driven by her political beliefs that she didn't have the freedom to sit back and read books on a Sunday afternoon. I don't want to be as driven as she's been," Jennifer says.

Lola tells me about the sixtieth birthday party that she and her sister arranged for their mother. "People came from all over the country. The tributes they made to her were incredible and beautiful, talking about how loving and nurturing and supportive she's been to them. Yes, I'd want her friends. And her daily professional achievement." But she also believes that her mother squandered too much of her strength and nurturance on other people. "It left her diminished. It left her with less energy for herself." She talks about the importance of "self-healing, self-loving experiences," which have not been part of her mother's life: "She's had to wait to be sixty to understand how important that is." That's the part of her mother's life that Lola doesn't want.

Anne-Marie reflects on the mother she knew in her early childhood. "I remember when I was about eight years old. She seemed to change so suddenly. She used to wear makeup and skirts and shave her legs. There was a sort of softness there that she put aside. It seemed like a real dislike of everything that had gone before. The things she chose to make political statements about have become personal. They're part of her now." Anne-Marie is perplexed about how to judge the changes. "I don't know why she pushed the softness away. I admire her ability to do that, I'm just not sure I want that for myself. I also worry that maybe she's given up parts of herself. Or maybe she's found herself, found what's really important to her."

The daughters reconstruct their mothers' lives from stories that evolve into family mythologies, from their memories of childhood and adolescence. As adults, they deconstruct those lives and extract from them a recurring theme upon which the details of their individual experiences are merely variations. Some daughters emphasize their mothers' struggle to be something other or more than wives and mothers. For some daughters economic struggle takes center stage. Others focus on the obstacles to professional achievement or failed love relationships. Some choose all of the above.

The theme is struggle. A few daughters embrace struggle because it is part of the human condition, but more important, because it enriches their lives. "I'm so glad my mother never hid her struggle from me. She's made me aware of the issues," says Maureen. "I'd rather that than go through life with blinders on." Ellie has absorbed not only the struggle, but also the excitement of her mother's life. "Her life has been great. So interesting. It still is. She loves her work, she travels and gives speeches, and obviously everyone thinks highly of her work. I really look up to her." And the struggle? Ellie waves her hand. "It's hard to be such a strong feminist. But who wants to go through life blissfully ignorant? It's always harder to be aware."

But for many of the daughters, struggle overshadowed the excitement. "Part of my mother's feminist struggle was the whole thing of entitlement and self-actualizing," Jane says. "Now she's stronger and confident, but it's too late because I wasn't there when she was feeling stronger. I was only there during her struggles."

Their mothers' lives were just too damned hard. That is why the daughters don't want their mothers' lives.

"The struggles she had!" Mary blurts out. "Economic struggles, work struggles. I want it to be easier for me."

Becky sums it up. "Would I want my mother's life if I could choose from all other lives? In a way. There's so much I admire. She's worked so hard and has gone through so many hard things. But no, I probably wouldn't want her life. I don't know if I'm made of the same stuff she is."

Although they're dubious about the struggle, the daughters admit that they love the rewards. "When I think of her life *now*, I could aspire to that," Ingrid says, speaking for most of the daughters. Rita, an African American daughter, says, "I think my mother is totally wonderful. But I don't want her life because it was harder than I want my life to be. I know we all go through our own really hard things. But I feel really fortunate that I'm twenty-two years after her." Like many of the daughters, Rita is confident that her life will be easier than her mother's, because her mother did some of the struggling for her. "I won't have to wait until I'm thirty to think, talk, and act on sexism and racism. I'll have that many years to develop it further. The path is easier."

But the daughters' stories are informed by a curious irony. It is precisely the process of struggle, the pioneering of new ways to be a woman, the overcoming of obstacles that the daughters observe with such wonder and admiration, that provide them with confidence about their own lives. The process that they reject is the source of their own strength and confidence, of the changes that have made their lives possible.

When Maria, thirty-three, talks about her mother, the word *struggle* appears over and over. She begins to laugh at herself. "There I go again, 'struggle.' " Maria has written for herself a life that looks like a complete rejection of what she calls her mother's "agenda." Her mother's agenda was for Maria to finish college, to be an activist in Latino and feminist causes, and to marry a Latino man. Maria did not finish college, has little interest in activism, and is a housewife married to a Caucasian man.

She reminisces about life in her mother's orbit: "We participated in strikes, we traveled, we performed in a Latino performing group, we sold our tapes and posters and records, we learned to silk-screen, and we met such interesting, important people. The exciting parts of my life were then, much more exciting than the life I've chosen now." She looks back on that life with affection—but no regrets. "Now life is mellow, and I love it. It's what I strive for." Maria unhesitatingly calls herself a feminist. She supports the right of women to choose their lives as she has chosen hers. "My mother is real supportive. She doesn't lay trips on me. I'm independent and shooting for my own happiness, like she shot for hers."

While Maureen, too, calls herself a feminist, her agenda is very different from Maria's and very much like her mother's. But she would certainly applaud Maria's gratitude to the mothers' generation for creating choices. "My mom has had a powerful effect on all of us, and we have so much respect for all she's done. I would want your book to include how great the mothers of all these daughters are. They've paved the road for all of us." They did it, Cary affirms, "by teaching us to love ourselves and to be proud to be a woman. It's great to have a mom who's not ashamed to be who she is."

CHAPTER SEVEN

Walking Your Talk: Where Are We Going and How Do We Get There?

Come along then, my sisters, unite with me, so that we do not remain behind while everything around and about us is pressing forward and struggling. . . . However, we shall also earn our part by not struggling in isolation—not everyone for herself, but rather everyone for all the others.

—LOUISE OTTO, *FRAUEN-ZEITUNG, EIN ORGAN FUR DIE HÖHEREN WEIBLICHEN INTERESSEN,* 1849

Nina tells a short story.

"My mother and I were sitting on the rim of the Grand Canyon, and we got into an intense discussion about the women's movement. She wanted to know where the women's movement is for my generation. 'We busted our asses so hard, so that your generation could have it so good, and you just let the women's movement drop. Why?' "

Nina answered her mother's question with one word: "Complacency."

A fitting conversation for the rim of the Grand Canyon. I can well imagine how the sight of endless crenellated peaks plunging to unimaginable depths and stretching out as far as the eye can see would provoke a feminist mother to ask such a question. Such sweep and beauty; so many obstacles.

Leaving the brave new world of her feminist family for a midwestern college in the autumn of 1990, Cary Atkins "assumed that the women in college would fight for their rights, because that's how I was brought up. But these women in my classes, they just accept the gains of the women's movement as part of their lives. They have happy lives, they can make money. They don't see the need for a women's movement to fight for equality." Cary is exasperated and indignant. "How can they believe that, when it was the women's movement that got them into college?"

Mia argues with her best friend, who says that "we have so much, why not just be comfortable?" She doesn't see the point of making trouble, trying to get more. "That is the attitude of a lot of women."

"We've slipped into this conservative era," Ellie observes, "reacting against things that were done in the sixties. People say, 'Well, women were feminists in the sixties, so now everything's OK.' "

I remember how the daughters attribute unpleasant connotations of the word *feminist* to "others," and wonder again whether such attribution is a displacement of their own attitudes. Is "other" women's complacency theirs as well?

The daughters are *not* complacent about the achievements of the women's movement. They celebrate the movement with a profound sense of gratitude. But gratitude hangs in a delicate balance with apprehension, for the movement's achievements are under siege. "I feel like we're getting more garbage thrown at us than ever before. We've very clearly gone backward, especially in the area of 'body image,' " Rachel says. "And abortion! Women are losing the control over their bodies that our mothers fought for."

"The advances for women made a huge leap when my mother and the women of her generation were fighting for them, like in the awareness of sexist laws," says Rita. "It's not that way now, and it is totally depressing. It's not that women are apathetic or that they have slacked off. It's that society's mind-set has changed."

That is dejection, not complacency.

As we saw in chapter three, the daughters thumb their noses at corporate values and are highly dubious of the rewards of corporate life. But the corporate take-over of the culture was only a partner in an elaborate dance. The daughters believe that in a curious and unexpected way the women's movement do-si-doed with the corporate mentality, creating not complacency but frenzy. In Suzanne Gordon's words, "Today, we believe that we must emulate the work and life-styles of the male—and now female—workaholics who sacrifice a personal, community, and civic life to the endless quest for more money, power, and status."

Rachel is a self-employed landscape gardener—a manual laborer, she calls herself. Her friends are more ambitious, "high-powered, more like my mother." Rachel says her friends hold feminist issues "in their minds and their hearts, and they hate being wrapped up in 'making it.' But the focus on financial betterment for women, the yuppie life-style, doesn't provide the time or energy for women's issues."

Linda, a film editor, finds her work demanding and fulfilling. She considers herself ambitious. "There are two parts of me. One is the person that has to cope in a dog-eat-dog world. I'm lucky just to survive, especially living in New York—let alone trying to change things. The other person is the real me. Deep inside I feel like, oh, there's so much I could do. I have so much to offer." She sighs. "Maybe at another point in my life. But right now I have too much."

Luz knows that her mother wants her to be more involved in feminist causes. "Come on, give me a break, I go to school full time, work thirty hours a week. Maybe I will be someday, but now I don't have the energy for things like that."

"Group work takes a lot of time and energy." Ingrid looks off into the distance. "It's hard to get from one week to another. If it wasn't such a struggle to make a living and get through life day by day, we might all have more energy for the overall ideals."

It's the times, the daughters say. The atrophying vitality of the women's movement is part of a larger gloomy picture.

"This whole country is falling apart," Linda says. "There's so much wrong in the whole world—crime, war, famine. What's wrong for women? Just throw it in there with everything else."

"I get to the end of four years of university—and I'm totally overwhelmed. All the racism and sexism and homophobia and classism. It's so complex, so entrenched. How are we ever going to do anything about it?" Rita despairingly asks.

The times. Too many issues. Too many problems. Too little clarity. Their mothers, the daughters believe, had clarity. "We look back on the civil rights movement, the feminist movement. It was obvious what the goals were," Shanna says. "My generation, we feel envious; like today the goals aren't so clear."

The waters have been muddied, in Ellie's view, by "insidious fake feminism, like you see in advertising and stuff." Ellie talks about television sitcoms and magazine ads that convey the message that "it's kind of OK for women to have careers and families as long as they're still 'feminine' and don't threaten men."

Fake feminism. Grace attends a university that still honors its reputation for student activism, however attenuated. She has been involved in student groups that address apartheid in South Africa, environmental problems, feminist and Latin American issues. She reports that "even in a community where things are more open to women on the surface, in reality they aren't." She finds gestures like choosing equal numbers of male and female speakers at student events to be formalistic concessions to women's demands for inclusion, still lacking in substance. "There are definitely problems for women doing these kinds of things. It's still a male-dominated atmosphere, even in the style of discourse. Interrupt and monopolize and prove—be macho. The male activists, no matter what they say, still monopolize. And it's true in classrooms, too."

Fake feminism. Shanna's circle of intimate friends is comprised of equal numbers of men and women. "I think men can be feminists. They can be allies, and I want men to be in our lives. All my male friends have feminist mothers, they all have good politics about feminism, and they *say* the right things. But when it comes to the women they're involved with, they're all emotionally and personally destructive. I can't figure it out."

Fake feminism. "It's even harder to deal with women's rights in the progressive community," says Hilary, "because the sexism is really subtle." She describes "men who call themselves feminists sitting right next to you making sexist jokes, like they're back in high school; sitting in a group with men and having them disregard you, looking to the other men for the answers. Then, when you raise it within these circles, the men ridicule you. How can we deal with it on the huge level when we can't even resolve it in small ways?"

Feminism languishes, the daughters say, not only because the times are harder and sexism is more subtle, but also because the women's movement has not kept its own house in order. The daughters of racial and ethnic minorities inhabit a separate room in the feminist house. They are doubly "other": other because they are not men and other because they are not white. This bond of fact and consciousness, however, does not make of them a homogeneous mass.

Luz is a Latina daughter. Her mother's adult working life began in a factory as she struggled to support her children and attend school. Luz works thirty hours a week to put herself through a community college. Her mother, now a social worker and leader of the community's Hispanic women's organization, is "annoyed" that Luz lacks a powerful identification with the Hispanic community, and Luz is annoyed that her mother "tries to push me into it." Luz's boyfriend is white; her other friends, male and female, span the rainbow.

Elaine, an African American daughter, has highly educated parents who hold well-paying, prestigious jobs, her mother at a university and her father in a corporation. Elaine "always attended private schools and had the best clothes." She is not attracted to white men, but, she says with a laugh, "You know that good old phrase, 'Some of my best friends are . . . ?' " One of her best friends is a white woman with whom she attended a state university, and another "really close friend" from high school also is a white woman.

Lola, an African American daughter of a mother family, grew up in a neighborhood ("working middle class, not yuppies or buppies") that lay in the shadow of a great eastern university. Her friends were from all corners of the world, but until the fifth grade she was the only black child in her school. Now, at age twenty-seven, she works at building a black community. Her friends, she says, are "fifty-fifty."

Maria's mother is Mexican American and her father Nicaraguan. Her stepfather is black. During her adolescence years Maria was a member of a Hispanic women's performing group, traveling throughout the West to support the grape workers' strikes and boycotts. Now Maria is married to a white man and lives in an affluent midwestern suburb.

Christine grew up in a white neighborhood and attended integrated schools. She chose to attend a black college because "I wanted that experience with my peers and people of my race." Now her social life is exclusively in the black community and in her black church.

Daughters of color and ethnic minorities come from all over the map of class—whatever that is in America. Several like Rita, who calls herself a mestizo, identify with more than one race, being Caucasian–African American, Caucasian-Hispanic, Caucasian-Asian. Some minority daughters grew up in completely white environments. Others grew up in homogeneous black or ethnic neighborhoods, later to be drawn out of these by school integration. For some, social life and work life have remained integrated. For others, as they entered the adult world, childhood and adolescent friendships with Caucasians became casual, episodic encounters. The family constellations of the daughters of color vary, as do their life experiences. But regardless of the forces of class, race, and experience that distinguish them from each other, regardless of the fact that they all are daughters of feminists, to a woman they experience race as a greater obstacle than gender to whatever they want from life.

The first daughter of color that I interview—she prefers to be anonymous—is succinct: "I'd rather be called a bitch than a nigger!" I repeat her statement to all the daughters of color when we talk about the relationship of race and gender.

"I'd rather not be called either," says Colette. "But if I had to choose . . . well, if you're called a bitch, that allows you to have intelligence, to have a heritage. You're still a person. But if you're called a nigger, you are *nothing*. You are chattel. You could have eighty million books under your belt, all the degrees in the world. You could be that amazing. And with that word somebody takes it all away from you."

"Do I understand you correctly?" I ask Lola. "Are you saying that the problematic areas in your life are not to do with being a woman but with being black?"

"That's too simplistic," Lola answers. She describes her experiences of sexual discrimination in a variety of work situations, like the one described in chapter three ("These *fucking* women. I'm just so *fucking* sick of work-

ing with you *fucking* women"). Then she offers a para-
ble. "Let's say a white woman goes to a restaurant. She
gets discourteous service; the food is crummy; everything
goes wrong. She complains to the manager. Let's say the
same thing happens to me. I don't complain to the manager. Because, frankly, what goes through my mind is not
that this is happening because I'm a woman. This is happening because I'm black."

"When I walk into a room, the first thing anyone
notices is my color," Elaine says. "People are always surprised that I'm smart and literate—that's not because I'm
a woman. And it's the same for men. A black man has a
harder time than a white man." Elaine tells me this in
several different ways to make sure I understand how
strongly she feels about it.

Curiously, the daughters' conviction that race impedes
more powerfully than gender is partly a consequence of
the triumphs of the women's movement. "Feminism is a
celebration," Lola says. "Racism is a problem." She reels
off a list of "effective" women's organizations. "They're
taking care of things and women are cognizant. But
the black community is so inundated with issues like
drugs. . . ." She throws up her hands. "So many things . . .
we're just not in concert. Maybe I'm naive, but I feel like
women are always in concert with each other."

Marcia says, with some caution, that "women are coming along. I'm not so optimistic about racial issues. I find
it so sad, so discouraging. After all we've gone through
for years and years, and all the lives that have been lost
and wasted—and we still have racial problems."

For Susanna, women's issues are not even a close second to racial issues. "It's not because I don't care about
sexism. Personally, I feel passionate about it when I'm

exposed to it." Then comes the clincher: "I think that because I grew up with a mom who was so empowered, it's not the issue that I automatically think of."

Lola points her finger at me. "Your daughters benefit from your consciousness without having had to develop the consciousness themselves. With black people," she says, careful to distinguish black people from "other races," "you have a different phenomenon. All the black people who were civil rights activists, who paved the way—and race is *still* more of an issue. That second-generation phenomenon of reaping the benefits of the foundation that someone laid for you is not possible for young black people."

I am acutely aware of how Lola, the daughter of a black feminist, has chosen her words to me, a white feminist mother; "*your* daughters." Lola calls feminism a celebration and she identifies herself unequivocally as a feminist. But she also points out that the feminist movement has "overwhelmingly, statistically benefited white women disproportionately to women of color. It enabled white women to become equally as problematic as their male counterparts." In other words, racist.

"If racism is in the whole society, it's going to be in women too," says Rita, adding that "white women have been so oppressed that I guess they seek out other people to oppress, like women of color."

The minority daughters agree that the feminist movement must own up to its culpability. Susanna, the child of a Caucasian father and an Asian mother, tells me she could easily "pass" as white because people usually think she is of Mediterranean heritage. But she identifies herself as a woman of color, and at thirty-two, she already has an impressive history of activism: at her university she was prominent in organizations of students of color; she has held key positions on the staffs of a local and a state politician; she has worked in the Asian community as a psychology intern and as a fund-raiser for a women's organization whose emphasis is on poor women and women of color. "I have to tell you frankly that the *word* feminism makes me think of racism. Betty Friedan and Gloria Steinem make me think of racism," she says.

I ask her whether anything in the mothers' generation of feminism is relevant to her life. Susanna ponders the question for a long time before she answers.

"I'm not sure I even want to think about where we'd be today without it. A lot was accomplished by the feminist movement."

She hesitates. I wait for the "but."

"I read *The Women's Room* by Marilyn French. I *totally* hated that book. I couldn't relate to any of it. I've never known a housewife. Most people of color have never known housewives. Our ancestors were workers."

Rita agrees. "Here you are reading all these feminist writers who are telling you to bust out of the kitchen and get into the work force. What does that have to do with the majority of women of color who have always been in the kitchen *and* the work force at the same time?"

The minority daughters, like the rest of the daughters, regard the right to work as a cornerstone of liberation for themselves as individuals and for all women. But they come at it from a different angle: not as "china dolls," in Shanna's words, but as descendants of women "who don't feel less oppressed because they work."

For all working-class women regardless of their color, work has meant neither fulfillment nor liberation. It means survival. Susanna believes that to resolve all forms of oppression, including the oppression of women, "there has to be more equitable allocation of resources, less of the rich and poor stuff." She points to reports on the feminization of poverty as "the way I relate to the oppression of women."

Many of the daughters think about poverty. But poverty and class are not exactly the same thing, and few daughters are prepared to grapple with class as even one explanation for disenfranchisement. Regardless of their racial and social origins, the daughters find class a slippery concept. Lola tells me that in spite of her life-long intimate friendships with Caucasian women, she experiences an instant flash of "understanding" with African Americans of both sexes that is lacking with white women.

I ask her to consider the following scenario: "You go into somebody's house and meet the cleaning woman. Nine times out of ten, if she's not Latina, she's black. Do you feel the same understanding with her?"

Lola tilts her head and regards me silently. Then she answers, "Hmmm . . . Well, I guess my first reaction is that I'm glad she's got a job. And, I mean, well . . ." Another long pause. "That's getting into class issues, isn't it? Well, that's hard for me to get a handle on."

Most of the daughters of color reproach feminism for its white face, even when they do so delicately. But like Susanna, who has not minced words, it is "less a criticism of feminist *issues* and more a criticism of the women's *movement*."

Rita calls herself a feminist, so it is hardly surprising that she celebrates the content of feminism. "I define myself as a woman identified with women, and I completely uphold the potential power of women. Sure, feminist issues mean something to women of color. Definitely. But why are all the women in feminist organizations white? A woman of color walking into a meeting of feminists is still going to see white women. So they don't see our faces, hear our stories, our version."

"The critical question," Susanna explains, "is not whether the women's movement was intentionally racist. But the movement ended up being white and middle-class, the leadership and the role models didn't apply to women of color. I can't believe in a movement that's supposed to address women but that doesn't involve all women."

Mary belongs to an association of professional and business women. "I went to the convention last year—all white women. They're all from the suburbs where the women are of their own color. They're not sensitive to women of color, because they don't know."

How should white women know, I ask? Some daughters of color believe that the initiative lies with white women. They must work toward their own perestroika.

"White women have to stop saying, 'Come, we pity you,' or 'We'll give you some time to hear you out—you'll fit in somewhere.' They should admit that they don't know what women of color need and say, 'Hey, we really need your input.' They should seek it out, and not on an individual token basis."

"White women just wait to be told about other women's experiences. I get so tired of always explaining. You have to rewrite your definitions of feminism to include women of color."

But the minority daughters are not letting themselves off the hook either.

"Minority women have to sort themselves out. When

minority women don't participate, white women can only say what they *think* we want."

"The only way you can start to change things is for women of color to be feminist and to be in feminist organizations. And to say, 'Look, we're feminists too.' "

"Black women's groups have struck out on their own. Maybe it's time for black and white women to work for things together."

Some women have benefited more from feminism than others, but all women still suffer from sexism. Just as they experience racism from white men *and* white women, the daughters of color experience sexism from white men *and* men of their own race or ethnicity. It's out there, big and bold, and it comes in all colors.

"I've run into sexism from black and white men equally," Mary says. "They're the MAN, they're the head. I'm supposed to be demure and sit back. It's a constant struggle." Lola's field, filmmaking, is dominated by white men, and she had imagined that working for a black man would be a different kind of experience—a better experience: "Oh, hallelujah, I'll be working for a black man!" She grimaces. "In fact, those have been some of the most problematic scenarios for me. The black men I've worked for are so condescending, so patronizing to me because I'm a woman. It pisses me off. I've had to leave jobs because of that."

Cynthia, a Latina daughter, was married at fifteen and divorced at eighteen. She describes her husband, also Hispanic. "He was like his father and all of his brothers. *Their* women had to stay home, cook, they couldn't work. He demanded that everything had to be done his way. They treated women like slaves."

"You know, men are egomaniacs. Both black and

white men," Christine says. "But black men have it hard. They can't get ahead as easily as black women." Like all the daughters of color, she alludes to the horrendous unemployment rate among men of color. "In the black community men put women down because they feel inferior," Elaine explains. "Black men are not as well educated as black women and they're unemployed. They feel bad about themselves, so they put women down. They stand on the street corner and when a woman walks by they yell, 'Hey, bitch!' "

"Black men are jealous of black women. I encounter that all the time." Christine is compassionate, but she is exasperated as well. "You have to boost their egos all the time. I'm telling you, it's a job! Never again will I get into a relationship where I have to downplay myself to boost him up. I've worked too hard to get where I am."

I ask the minority daughters, women subject to the double whammy of racism and sexism, which issue engages their time and energy. They choose not to choose. Jennifer believes that women's organizations and minority organizations are equally flawed. "People of color have rejected feminism because it hasn't recognized issues of race as well as it could have. Movements against racism and for civil rights have neglected women as well. None of us is perfect yet, but I'm not about to deny either part of me."

But listen, I insist. You have to make choices in life. Where do you choose to put your efforts? Women's issues? Issues of race? "At this point, I'd go for the black issues—especially because I think they need a feminist perspective." Have Feminism, Will Travel, is Jennifer's solution.

It is Colette's solution, too. Colette, age twenty-two,

is an African American daughter now attending medical school. "I'll work in the black community. I wouldn't feel right if I took myself out of it. But I can't separate race and gender. I can't wash away my color and I can't wash away my femininity." So, she will take her feminism into the black community. "Black women would get that positive female role model—and black men, too."

"It's not a conflict for me," says Mary. "No matter what color I am, I'm a woman first. I face more problems than white women do in this society . . . but being a woman is being a woman. Women pulling together—that's what it's all about."

Shanna expresses a hope voiced by many daughters of color that stems from a proud historical consciousness. "Today people talk more about racial issues than feminist issues. Race is a big deal in the media now. But look at the feminist movement! It came after the civil rights movement. Maybe it'll happen that way again."

Many daughters, regardless of race or ethnicity, stir feminist issues into the great cauldron of what they call human issues. When Holly was twelve she marched in a gay rights parade with her mother. "I was like, oh Mom, why do we have to be here? My mom said it was about civil rights." The event sticks fast in Holly's mind. "I'm a feminist, but being a feminist is also respecting equal rights for everyone. Otherwise feminism is too narrow. I certainly hope I don't run into feminists who are members of the KKK. Sure, you're for women's agendas and issues, but there are other people who have the same issues."

Judith, a law student, squarely sets women's issues into

the global social and political context. "We need free abortion on demand, socialized medicine, houses for everyone to live in; we need public transportation and peace in the Middle East. The connection between empowering women and these issues—that's my grand scheme."

Elaine has a double major in Women's Studies and Afro-American Studies because she wants to "know my history." She is not a joiner and she does not anticipate a life of activism. "It's not necessarily good, but I'm more the type to send a check." Her causes of choice? "Children. I'd give to the March of Dimes, or to AIDS research or to helping the homeless. I'm certainly race and gender conscious, but it's not my only focus. There's more to life."

"I think of feminism as a humanistic value, as a celebration of people, of giving people respect and opportunities, regardless of male, female, black, white. I take it further than just gender," says Renata.

First, second, or mixed in there with everything else that needs mending, reform, or remaking in our society, women's issues still cry out for attention, and the daughters agree that there is yet far more to do than has already been done. The problems they regard as unsolved or half-solved fly in all directions, each daughter with her own special twist and emphasis: reproductive rights, pay equity, child care, feminized poverty, parental leave, political representation, occupational representation, sexual harassment, and generic sexism in every corner and crevice of the social edifice. In short, every issue any feminist mother ever thought about—except one large, messy, issue.

The concept of woman-as-sex-object, never a tidy package at best, has fragmented into its component parts.

And none of the parts are high on the daughters' list of burning issues. Curious, isn't it, when we consider the daily conflict, indeed agony, that many of the daughters experience over weight (first and foremost) and over crossing the line between decorating themselves for pleasure and succumbing to sexist dictates of beauty. But as we saw in chapter four, some daughters believe that when women evaluate other women by "externals," they are simply doing what men do, albeit from a different perspective. They strive to avoid that trap. Collectively they fume at how the media relentlessly promotes and buttresses sexist standards of beauty; individually they resist blindly conforming to those standards. Yet, as Jennifer puts it, "when it comes right down to it, things like shaving legs are low on the list." Grappling with sexist standards of beauty is a matter of private choice for the daughters. It is somehow not worthy of public debate.

And some daughters are just worn out. When Rachel shaves her legs and perms her hair for the first time in her twenty-eight years, she feels like a traitor to feminist principles. She also feels relieved; "In some ways making statements against all that stuff has been as controlling as giving in to it."

The mothers' generation discerned a continuum beginning with the tyranny of beauty and ending at violence against women. The logical conclusion of construing women's bodies as objects for male pleasure, the mothers believed, is women's bodies as objects of male hostility. The continuum, straight and true for the mothers, dips and curves for the daughters.

Anne-Marie, like all daughters, is deeply offended that "I can't walk where I want to by myself, that I have to be very careful about making eye contact on the streets, that

I have to worry about how I dress, how I look." Yet there is a break in the continuum when I ask about the implications of their individual experiences for the larger realm of women's common discomforts.

Many feminists of the mothers' generation equated pornography with violence against women; the equation is not so clear to the daughters. In fact, when I ask the daughters what issues remain to be resolved, pornography rarely comes up spontaneously. The issue flaps about at the outer edges of concern for them, making a little breeze but hardly a wind. "I don't really see how pornography encourages exploitation of women. I don't get that one," Ingrid shakes her head. "I guess it should bother me, but it doesn't. If a woman wants to participate in it, it's her choice. And if you don't like to see women in that way, then you don't have to look."

"I think it's terrible and wrong, and I don't know what to do about it," says Amy. "So, I've just chosen to be in a world where I don't have to deal with it." Amanda finds pornography "disgusting," but like Amy, "I don't pay attention to it. I don't approve of it, so I stay away from it. When I'm confronted by it, I look away." End of discussion.

While pornography does not spring to mind as a hot topic for discussion, the daughters do not dismiss it when I bring it up. They recognize it for the messy business that it is. "It certainly has an effect on people," Shanna says. "But it's not like a man sees a magazine picture and says now I'm going to go out and rape a woman. It's that it reinforces the attitude that women are there just as sexual things." While that's not good, she adds, "I think erotica is healthy."

Having inherited a claim to their full sexuality, the

daughters are wary of undermining it by rejecting the erotic. And if it is difficult to prove that pornography stimulates, or is synonymous with, violence against women, it is often no easier to distinguish the erotic from the pornographic. "I really dislike violent pornography that has pain in it. But sexuality is really important." Judith rambles a bit, trying to figure out for herself the difference between pornography and erotica. "Hard-core, like *Hustler,* no. And I don't want to see nude calendars on the wall where I work. But the catalogue for Victoria's Secret is fine. I even think that women can use that catalogue to explore their own erotic side."

"I don't like to see women presented as sexual orna-ments, like there's nothing to them but their bodies. But I also think there's nothing wrong with the naked body. Where do you draw the line?" Ingrid wonders.

Wherever they draw the line between pornography and erotica, and whether or not they are convinced that por-nography is equivalent to violence against women, the daughters are appalled at depictions of women submit-ting to violence. Doing something about it is as tricky as defining it.

The slightest suggestion of censorship evokes a re-sounding "No!" "Pornography?" Adrienne asks. "Bla-tant pornography all over the place is inappropriate, but I'm a civil libertarian. If people want to buy it, they should have that right."

Liza is impatient with picky distinctions between hard-core and soft porn. They are equally unacceptable to her because "it makes men think they can treat women in certain ways—and it makes women see themselves that way. But I'm against banning it. That's a freedom-of-choice issue."

Censoring pornography is picking up the wrong end of the stick. Judith has trouble deciding which is worse—"hurting people, if pornography does that, or inhibiting freedom of speech." She decides that on balance it is more important to defend civil liberties, especially since in the end, "if we banned pornography, men would find a way to buy it and just carry it around in plain brown paper." Heather, too, is convinced that "taking it off the stands doesn't solve anything. We have to look at the way kids are raised."

Emily "can't stand pornography. I make it a big issue with boyfriends. I tell them it's just not going to exist around me." Liza, vehemently against any kind of censorship, agrees: "If the men we care about read *Playboy,* we tell them that it's not acceptable, and we stop being friends with them. That's how you regulate it. You take away the market."

The daughters opt for the long, slow haul, for the private rather than the public approach. Get your own relationships in shape! Educate your own boyfriends! And they have another word for women as well: get your own act together. Among the daughters' unexpected responses, none astonished me as much as the opinion that women are as responsible for pornography as men.

Mary tells me that she hates MTV. "I think these women put themselves in a terrible position."

Put themselves?

"OK, so they've been enticed, but I don't know if I'd call them victims. They make a choice."

"What I really don't like is child pornography. A child has no choice," Elaine says. "But the adult woman? She's making a choice. Maybe she'll make more money taking her clothes off than she will as a waitress. Maybe she needs the money to pay her rent and feed her kids. Same thing with a prostitute." Elaine grows pensive. "But then I think—you're being pimped by a man. How can you be doing that?"

Luz is "totally against pornography. But the woman who does it, that's what she *wants* to do, that's how she wants to portray herself. But it gives other women a bad name."

If woman-as-sex-object is a footnote to the daughters' agendas, reproductive rights is written at the top in bold letters, underlined. Devotion to reproductive rights transcends race, ethnicity, life experience, and religion. The daughters' consensus on abortion is total, complete, undeviating.

"It's not a moral issue. It's *the* most important thing," Shanna asserts, "because it's a matter of life and death." She is not talking about the death of a fetus, but about women who died from botched underground abortions in the "old country," as Amelia calls prefeminist times, and about women who may do so again in the new world order. She is also talking about the death of the aspirations of women who bear unwanted children.

Most of the daughters are impatient with moral arguments against abortion. But four of the African American daughters are deeply religious, and for two of them the church is the center of their social universe. Christine was brought up in the church "from the get-go"; its teachings inform every aspect of her world view. Her support of a woman's right to choose abortion does not come easily. "I've thought about it a lot," Christine sighs. She speaks of psychological pain, she talks about taking a life.

"It's horrible. But we've talked about it in this house, about how men don't have to make the choice of whether to have an abortion for themselves, but they get to make the decisions for women. We say women should have the choice. It's a woman's body."

Cynthia's parents, Puerto Rican Americans, were both Pentecostals. Her father remained in the church, her mother abandoned it. Cynthia wonders "what would happen if abortion was to become illegal again, like back in the sixties, when you had to do all those crazy things to have an abortion." For herself, she is torn. "I always think, what would I do if I got pregnant and didn't want the child or couldn't support it? I'd go crazy trying to make that decision," because she believes that "abortion is taking a life." But she is unshakably prochoice. "A woman has the right to decide for herself. She has to do what she has to do."

What does a woman have to do about any of the issues half-resolved or unresolved? Nina calls herself a feminist, "but at the same time, for me to be an environmentalist is almost more important. Without the earth to take care of us, things like affirmative action, women's rights—they won't matter." She is not, however, recommending that women wait until the earth is all healed and secure to take care of women's business. How should women take care of business, I ask? Nina answers, "Through their own actions and their own behavior—you know, walking your talk."

That covers a lot of territory. For Nina walking your talk means "calling men on their behavior. Like, hey, you're being a jerk! You're blowing it. It means standing up to the patriarchy when it starts to shoot you down. You know what I mean?"

This is what it means to Olivia. She spent several years with a crew in the California mountains, rehabilitating trails and enhancing streams and salmon environments. Olivia and the few other women on the crew were given the "crap jobs," digging ditches with a shovel while men used the grip hoists and the chain saws. "The other women took on this submissive role. I was the one who went around and preached about not taking on that role. It became my mission." She took on the men as well. "Finally, one day I said to this sexist supervisor, 'You're sexist, I won't work with you anymore.'" Olivia got what she wanted: a different supervisor, the chain saw, the grip hoist, the respect. "I proved to myself that if I'm persistent, I can get what I need. My mother taught me that you don't sit around and wait. That's a feminist thing for me."

"You do it from the ground up," Adrienne counsels. "From inside your own little family—like with the one man whose mind you can change—or the company you work for, changing the minds of the people around you."

"People are set in what they believe," Becky says. "I've had more talks with people about women's issues. It doesn't matter what you say to them, they're set." She is not despondent, however. "A woman president is a long way down the line. But if I do my part in my own life, and other people do their part, we can get there."

A firm, unbroken thread of individual responsibility and individual efficacy runs through the daughters' ruminations about how to address pervasive sexism: Deal with it in your own backyard. "You know, the thing about practicing what you preach," Jenna points out. "How can you argue for something if you're not practicing it?"

That's the good news. Shanna points out that "we can work on feminist issues in anything we're involved in. We don't have to confine ourselves to majoring in Women's Studies. We can take it with us." Christine does just that. As a second-grade teacher of a predominantly black class, sexism in children's literature is on her mind. "Like Cinderella, she's in rags and she has to dress up a certain way to get a man. If you're one of the ugly stepsisters, a man won't look at you. I don't read stuff like that to the kids."

When I interview Liza, she has just finished writing a novel. "My job as a writer is to be responsible and never write anything sexist—or racist or ageist." Maureen is preparing for graduate studies in demography. She loves demography as an intellectual discipline that has fascinating implications for the study of women. As a teacher she hopes to be a model for women students and to teach all students "from a feminist perspective."

The troubling news is that for some daughters individual responsibility is the end point as well as the beginning. Amanda has "spent a lot of time thinking about women in the workplace. I believe that if I'm positive, I'll be treated that way. I'll make sure, and I always have, that I'm treated fairly. It's more of a personal mission. It takes place personally."

"I can make my own life," Luz says. "I carve out my own wonderful life. See, that's what my mother taught me."

The daughters have learned that half of the mothers' lessons well. Sometimes experience teaches them the other half. Dealing with women's issues alone in your own backyard is not always easy or effective. Anne-Marie has been working with computers for years and is currently the assistant systems operator at her firm, supervising seven people. "One day my boss said right in front of me, 'We'll have to get someone in here who really understands the system.' I was, like, *excuse me?* I was so shocked that I couldn't say anything. It happens all the time, but I never tell him off. I'd like to be more assertive, but he's my boss, you know."

"I sometimes act like a wimp," says Mary. Some years ago when she held a supervisory position in a firm, she attended a meeting with two male superiors to discuss a project that she had initiated and supervised. "So we're sitting there and I start to interject—and one of my bosses turns to me and says, 'Shut up!' The nerve of him!" Mary tells the story laughing, but she stops when she softly adds, "I shut up! When I look back on it, I know I should have walked out, I should have done this or that. I didn't know how."

Maureen attends a Catholic university. Her professor of religious philosophy "refers to God as 'He' and 'Him.' I raised my hand one day and said, 'I'm very uncomfortable with that because my god is not he and him.' And he said, 'Well, that's too bad. I'm a traditionalist and that's how I talk.' Basically he was telling me to deal with it. So I have to sit there and struggle to adjust every word he says in my mind."

It happens to the daughters all the time in the classroom, at work, in social situations, in personal relationships. Cultivating one's own garden is a lonely business. I suggest to the daughters that it's also a pretty slow way to do things; office by office, classroom by classroom, mate by mate.

The issue of reproductive rights brazenly trumpets a different sound, piercing the daughters' certitude that they can get what they need by their individual efforts. Amanda has barged into a profession—industrial design—in which women are still scarce as hen's teeth. She regales me with one anecdote after another of the sexist assumptions and behavior of first her male teachers and fellow students and now her male colleagues. She is utterly confident that with her talent, perseverance, optimism, and her tactic of silence she will overcome and get the prize—fulfilling, creative work and recognition. The last thing in the world she looks for is "getting anyone else involved" in her "personal mission" as a woman making her way in a man's world. Amanda abhors confrontation.

Then we talk about reproductive rights, and Amanda immediately switches gears. Without missing a beat she begins to talk about collective action and, if need be, confrontation.

The daughters see with utmost clarity that abortion rights are not a prize that a woman, whatever her personal merits, can win in reasonable discourse with her physician. First among women's issues for the daughters, the right to reproductive choices is like a wake-up call. But it is a lonely sound that resonates only feebly beyond that issue.

I ask the daughters whether they remember the slogan, "The personal is political." They rummage around in memory's attic, dusting off this and that piece of memorabilia. When they find the slogan, it is barely recognizable. Their commitment to feminist goals—so strong in private life—falters in the public realm.

To be sure, many daughters agree with Judith that

"there is more power in numbers." Rita, who staunchly believes that to resolve women's issues "it has to come from the inside first," also believes that individual consciousness must advance to the level of public consciousness. "It needs to be left and center; legislative, political, legal stuff. It has to deal with people's feelings and how they see things." Debby concludes that "sexism is so pervasive that it's hard to know where to begin. I guess everywhere at once. In the family, in the workplace, in the churches, in politics. Even in the UN—sexism is international."

These daughters walk their talk in a larger social arena. Judith describes a professor who "consistently made sexist and racist comments" in a class at her law school. "We women students waged a sustained campaign to get him taken off the first-year curriculum, because first-year students can't choose the courses they take. He's no longer teaching first-year courses." Rita dreams of writing nonsexist children's textbooks, and in the meantime she works on a citizens' review board to investigate how the police treat women, the homeless, and people of color. Nicole raises funds for a local prochoice organization. Debby is the founder of a feminist bisexual women's organization. Lola organizes a group of women in the film industry. And all of the daughters agree with Liza that it is of the utmost importance "to keep thinking about the issues."

"When there's a call, I respond," Rita says. Some daughters do respond, but few think of themselves or act as initiators in the public realm. Liza tells me, as so many daughters do, "I participate in marches, but I don't organize them. I feel responsible and I give a strong feminist message. But I'm not an organizer." When someone hands the daughters a petition on women's issues, they eagerly, gladly sign. They write letters to legislators. They march in demonstrations and many give money. Every daughter who has taken part in some kind of collective endeavor has experienced a rush of exultation. Rita speaks for them: "It's so great to be there with other women who care."

So, like Nina's mother, I wait for the daughters to talk Movement. A few do articulate their longing for a "movement" to rise from the detritus of backlash, complacency, individual solutions, and the speed-up culture.

Maureen laments that "it's so rare to meet a woman who shares my beliefs, who's grown up in a feminist environment like I did." But Maureen wants more than a buddy. "I know that the only way women made a difference in the past was collectively. I get so frustrated, thinking about how great the sixties were, when women did, you know, work collectively. I feel so deprived of those collective things."

"The first thing is for women to reclaim that they are an issue. I think it's still a dirty word, feminism," Hilary says. She is pessimistic about making gains without a movement. "As long as we don't participate in electoral politics, the women who get through are the women that the boys let get through. There has to be a women's movement that supports women politicians who support women's issues." She casts about for good signs. "The issues of choice, sexual harassment, all the stuff coming down the road at us. It's slapping us in the face and we can't just sit on our asses. I think a movement is coming up from under cover."

Daughters like Maureen and Hilary yearn for a feminist home, for a way to express themselves in collective action. "I know how to support a woman on an individual level, but I don't know what to do about it on a larger level. I've got all the feelings, but I don't know where to put them," says Anne-Marie. The great epiphany of the mothers' movement, collective involvement, seems to have become an art, accessible only to the skilled practitioner.

Amelia feels helpless and frustrated. "You guys went through the movement together. You could come out and say, 'We're feminists. Let's unite.' "

"Why can't you?" I ask.

"Because women of my age haven't gone through that empowerment. It happened when we were too young to be involved."

The women's movement triumphantly elevated female "personal" experience from the unworthy and the trivial to a high level of importance in the culture. The issues may often be distorted, co-opted, and reviled, but they are discussed on talk shows and on the editorial pages of large and small newspapers, in books that tumble forth from the pens of the mothers' and the daughters' generations. The issues have become the stuff of soap operas and literature. They are debated in the courts and the legislatures. Women's issues have become part of the public discourse in our time. The daughters rejoice that the mothers made it so. Even the daughters of color who find much wanting in the feminist movement nonetheless honor the goals and gains of feminism.

The women's movement emerged and evolved in a visionary atmosphere, the same atmosphere that nurtured other movements that dreamed about making all relationships new. Times change and visions change. I cannot think of a single great social movement that has handed down to its successors the élan of its creators. Like much else in that visionary period, the sweeping utopianism that framed the mothers' movement has splintered. While the daughters hold fast to the fragments, for them feminism does not consistently cohere into a whole vision. But even in its fragmented state, feminism continues to inform their lives.

True, some daughters qualify the word before they call themselves feminists, and many have reordered the importance of this or that feminist issue. But they pursue fulfillment—as women—with the strength, confidence, and resolution that their mothers wished for them. The daughters carry the mothers' legacy into their personal relationships with both women and men. The mothers' legacy of broad social commitment powerfully influences their choices of occupation. However private their pursuits, the daughters recognize that it is not enough to simply give some women a larger slice of a defective pie. That is why the daughters won't vote for a woman—just because she is a woman—if she does not uphold women's rights or minority rights or gay and lesbian rights.

The task for women, mothers and daughters alike, is different and perhaps more difficult now than it was when the mothers were young. Every day the mothers were buoyed by the recovery of another long-buried or never-acknowledged heroine. Every day the mothers had another exhilarating insight about how so-called human values were masculine values, and yet another revelation about how one need not be trapped by those values. The mothers, succored by that experience and those memories, are nonetheless as vulnerable to current realities as the daughters. For today the discoveries and insights spill out of the feminist cornucopia into a social, political, and economic atmosphere that is hostile to dreams of social transformation. In such a world, as Rita says, "It isn't enough to be born into feminism as I was. You have to make a decision to be conscious of it and to stick to it. You have to make it happen."

WORKS CITED

· · · · · · · · · · ·

Bateson, Mary Catherine. *Composing a Life*. New York: Plume/Penguin, 1990.

Boswell, James. *Boswell's Life of Johnson*. New York: E. P. Dutton, 1968.

Brittain, Vera. *Lady into Woman*. London: A. Dakers, 1953.

Burton, Gabrielle. *I'm Running Away from Home but I'm Not Allowed to Cross the Street*. Pittsburgh: Know, Inc., 1972.

Chodorow, Nancy. *The Reproduction of Mothering*. Berkeley: University of California Press, 1978.

De Beauvoir, Simone. *The Second Sex*. New York: Alfred A. Knopf, 1953.

Ehrenreich, Barbara, and Deirdre English. *For Her Own Good: 150 Years of the Experts' Advice to Women*. New York: Anchor Books, 1979.

Eliot, George. *Adam Bede*. New York: Penguin Books, 1980.

Faludi, Susan. *Backlash*. New York: Crown Publishers, 1991.

Gordon, Suzanne. *Prisoners of Men's Dreams*. Boston: Little, Brown & Co., 1991.

Gould, Stephen Jay. *The Mismeasure of Man*. New York: W. W. Norton, 1981.

Havel, Vaclav. "Words on Words." *New York Review of Books.* January 18, 1990, 20–21.

Heilbrun, Carolyn G. *Writing a Woman's Life.* New York: W. W. Norton, 1988.

———. *Hamlet's Mother and Other Women.* New York: Columbia University Press, 1990.

Le Guin, Ursula K. *Dancing at the Edge of the World.* New York: Harper and Row, 1990.

Martin, Del, and Phyllis Lyon. *Lesbian/Woman.* California: Volcano Press, 1991.

Mencken, H. L. *In Defense of Women.* New York: Alfred A. Knopf, 1918.

Otto, Louise. *Frauen-Zeitung, Ein Organ fur die höheren weiblichen Interessen,* 1849. As cited in *Women, the Family, and Freedom. Volume I: 1750–1880* by Susan Groag Bell and Karen Offen. Stanford: Stanford University Press, 1983.

Rich, Adrienne. *Blood, Bread, and Poetry.* New York: W. W. Norton, 1986.

———. *Of Woman Born.* New York: W. W. Norton, 1986.

———. *On Lies, Secrets, and Silence.* New York: W. W. Norton, 1979.

Rubin, Lillian B. *Erotic Wars: What Happened to the Sexual Revolution.* New York: Farrar, Straus & Giroux, 1990.

Sidel, Ruth. *On Her Own: Growing Up in the Shadow of the American Dream.* New York: Penguin Books, 1990.

Walters, Suzanna Danuta. *Lives Together/Worlds Apart.* Berkeley: University of California Press, 1992.

Wolf, Naomi. *The Beauty Myth.* New York: William Morrow & Co., 1991.